THE WED

MW00619729

THE
WEDDING *of*
SOPHIA

The Divine Feminine in Psychoidal Alchemy

JEFFREY RAFF

NICOLAS-HAYS, INC.
Berwick, Maine

First published in 2003 by
Nicolas-Hays, Inc.
P. O. Box 1126
Berwick, ME 03901-1126

Distributed to the trade by
Red Wheel/Weiser, LLC
P. O. Box 612
York Beach, ME 03910-0612
www.redwheelweiser.com

Cataloging-in-Publication Data available on request at the Library of Congress

VG

Cover design and typesetting by Sky-Peck Design
Typeset in 10/13 Minion

Printed in the United States of America

09   08   07   06   05   04   03
7   6   5   4   3   2   1

The paper used in this publication meets the minimum requirements of the
American National Standard for Information Sciences—Permanence of Paper for
Printed Library Materials Z39.48–1992 (R1997).

Dedication

To Glen Carlson and Arnold Mindell—both in their own ways have contributed to the writing of this book and, more importantly, have given me the priceless gift of friendship.

CONTENTS

ACKNOWLEDGMENTS

My deepest thanks go to those individuals whose generous support, financial and otherwise, allowed me to find the time to write this book. You know who you are and you know how much I appreciate your generosity.

I also wish to express my gratitude to Lydia Lennihan, whose suggestions about the book helped me turn it into a far better work than it otherwise would have been. Thanks also to Valerie Cooper for her patience in helping me through some of the bad times and her efforts at editing. Lastly, I am grateful to my wife Marilyn, who survived the shock at discovering she married a mystic, and whose partnership only gets better with each passing year.

The following sources were used for the illustrations that appear in this book:

Michael Maier's Atalanta Fugiens: Sources of an Alchemical Book of Emblems by H. M. E. de Jong (York Beach, ME: Nicolas-Hays, 2002), figures 1, 2, 10. *The Hermetic Museum: Alchemy and Mysticism* by Alexander Roob (New York, Taschen, 1997), figures 3-9.

INTRODUCTION

Then, again, thou sayest that the Stone is prepared of one thing, of one substance, in one vessel, the four [elements] composing one essence in which is one agent which begins and completes the work; man, thou sayest, need do nothing but add a little heat, and leave the rest to thy wisdom.

—JEAN DE MEHUNG, *The Remonstrance of Nature*

A few years ago I awoke in the middle of the night to discover a being of transcendent beauty, surrounded by bright light, sitting on my bed. She told me that her name was Sophia, and she asked me to write a book about her. She gave me suggestions about how to write this book, and we talked for many hours. As is usual with such experiences, I could never recall all that she had told me, because I was in an altered state of consciousness and in another reality; the reality of the imagination. But I did remember her request to write this book, and the last thing she said to me. She asked me to show people that she was real, and that all the beings of the imagination are real. This book is my attempt to fulfill her request. Since I have studied alchemy for many years, I shall communicate the reality of Sophia through the alchemical language.

There was an alchemist who lived 800 years ago who also experienced Sophia and attempted to describe her in alchemical terms. His name is still unknown to us for certain, but his book is called *The Aurora Consurgens*. Writing in parables and with many references to alchemical processes, the author of *Aurora* ecstatically paints his love for Sophia and, in the culmination of the book, describes her marriage to the masculine side of God and to the alchemist, himself. I realized that I could use the *Aurora* text to convey my own experience of Sophia and her wedding. Rather than analyze all of the *Aurora*, I have worked with only those aspects of it that relate to Sophia's nature and the alchemical processes by which she weds.

Sophia, as I experienced her, and as I suspect the author of *Aurora* did as well, did not belong to my psyche, but was a transcendent being that belonged to the realm I have called, in earlier writings, "the psychoid."[1] The alchemy that concerns psychoidal entities such as Sophia and the processes that they undergo I have termed "psychoidal alchemy."

In psychoidal alchemy, as in all alchemy, though we use many terms and descriptions, we are talking about one mysterious entity. We may call this entity God, the *prima materia*, or many other terms. The essence about which this book speaks can never truly be explained; but it can be experienced and transformed, and through its transformation, transform others in turn. Sophia, though a psychoidal figure in her own right, is an aspect of this One Thing.

Every process of alchemy and every operation performed involve this One Thing. This is the Philosopher's Stone, the secret of all secrets and the magic of all magic. The Philosopher's Stone starts out in an undifferentiated and chaotic condition. The alchemist must discover the true nature of the *prima materia*, subject it to certain procedures, and then differentiate its components. These components consist of a number of pairs of opposites, depicted as the mysterious sulfur and mercury or often as the king and queen. The last pair of opposites is very appropriate for us because, in many ways, Sophia is the queen who is separated from the One Thing and married to the king, who is also derived from the primal unity.

In psychoidal alchemy we are dealing with forces and entities that transcend the psyche. They belong to another dimension of reality, which is neither purely physical nor purely psychic, but a mixture of the two. They live an imaginal reality between the world of spirit and the ordinary world. The imagination with which we perceive and work with psychoidal beings is not the usual imagination but a special one that the Sufis called the "Gnostic imagination." Sophia as queen and her spouse, the king, belong to the psychoid world and may therefore only be experienced through the Gnostic imagination, which I will discuss later.

In the world of spirit, God is undivided and, as such, I term it the godhead or the One Thing. Wishing to make itself known, it breaks up its own unity and manifests within the psychoid in a variety of forms, or Names. In psychoidal alchemy, we can say that the godhead is the *prima materia*, the divine essence with which the work begins, but alchemy only starts when the godhead manifests. Sophia is a manifestation of the godhead in the psychoid realm, and as such she has many meanings and functions, and creates a multitude of experiences for those lucky enough to know her. She is the feminine manifestation of the undifferentiated godhead and when she manifests, her opposite, masculine counterpart manifests as well. We shall call him "God" in this book, but shall not study him in detail. As the manifestation of the godhead, Sophia is the *prima materia*, the beginning of the work, and through her marriage she creates the end product of the work: the Philosopher's Stone.

Since alchemy first separates the opposites and then reunites them, Sophia must marry her masculine partner. The union of the opposites creates the Philosopher's Stone, so that the wedding of Sophia creates this ultimate mystery. Beginning with the godhead who of its own free will manifests in the psychoid realm as Names, which are understood as the divinity's manifestations of its own opposites, psychoidal alchemy proceeds to work with these opposites first separately, and then to conjoin them. Their marriage creates the stone, which is the divinity transformed and made unique. Beginning with the unknowable and impersonal One Thing, we end with the incarnation of an individuating God unique to ourselves. This is accomplished through the wedding of Sophia.

In my earlier writings I have demonstrated that the Stone is the equivalent of what I have termed the ally, a psychoidal being that incarnates the essence of the divinity in a unique and personal fashion. The ally is the child of Sophia and God, and is known to the alchemists as the *filius*. There are many psychoidal figures such as Sophia, but in the end they are all faces of the divine. We are just beginning to explore the psychoid, but I am already certain that it holds many different kinds of energies and beings that should one day be differentiated. The highest of all of these beings may be called gods and goddesses, or what the Sufis and Kabbalists called Names.

There are many reasons why I have chosen to combine the two themes of Sophia and psychoidal alchemy in this work; the most important is that Sophia governs nature and is responsible for processes of incarnation and transformation. In order to understand psychoidal alchemy, it is necessary to understand the feminine principal that underlies it. The *Aurora Consurgens* (the "Rising Dawn") is a particularly appropriate illustration of psychoidal alchemy because it deals at length with the figure of Wisdom, or Sophia, and affords great insight into her nature. I chose it as well because it was a text studied by one of my teachers — Dr. Marie Louise von Franz.[2] Written as a companion piece to C. G. Jung's greatest work on alchemy, *Mysterium Coniunctionis*,[3] her book remains a fine example of the psychological study of alchemy. Without disavowing von Franz's commentary (and, in fact, making much use of it), I approach this text from the different perspective of psychoidal alchemy. Finally, I fixed on this book because of its title, which for me announces the beginning of a new dawn of a new time, the time in which spiritual realities find their place in the hearts and minds of the individual.

I shall discuss a conception of spiritual realities that may seem strange to many readers. In my previous book on alchemy I tried to lay the groundwork for understanding the psychoid realm, psychoidal figures, and psychoidal alchemy. I demonstrated that the Jungian model was in fact a spiritual model that offered new insights about the nature of enlightenment and inner experiences most appropriate for contemporary Western culture. In that work, I presented such themes as the psychoid realm and the reality of psychoidal figures that did not belong to the human psyche. I shall develop these themes in particular in the current work and shall present alchemy as the confrontation and transformation of psychoidal figures—a series of encounters and operations of psychoidal alchemy. In so doing I have as my primary goal the exposition of the idea that psychoidal figures are real entities with a life and consciousness of their own, independent of the human soul. Moreover, the human being may not only encounter these figures, but also may enter into deep relationship with them: a relationship of mutual transformation.

Alchemy is about many things and is a system of thought and spiritual perceptions so rich and multileveled that no one explanation can do it justice. There is nothing either more humorous or sadder than the fevered attempt of certain writers on alchemy to prove that their point of view is the correct one. The truth is that alchemy portrays a mystery or mysteries about the nature of reality, matter, spirit, and other realms between these two. Moreover, alchemy has existed for two millennia and thousands of thinkers have contributed to its development. Though there are some who argue that the greatest of these thinkers knew exactly what they were writing about and were all in agreement about the true nature of alchemy, this seems most unlikely to me. The alchemists were individualistic and though they all, for the most part, use the same vocabulary, their intent and meaning was not always the same. Some current writers take the historical perspective of attempting to decipher the meaning of earlier alchemists. That is not my intent. Rather, I approach the symbolic expressions of alchemy from my own perspective and see in them a portrayal of the mysteries that concern me the most. Anyone who studies alchemy from other than the historical perspective is doing just this: finding in its images the mystery that grips them. I make no apology for this approach and I shall not enter into fruitless debate about what the true nature of alchemy is. Alchemy is a living sys-

tem and its symbols continue to evolve. Since it is concerned with mysteries that remain beyond our grasp, there is no way to exhaust the creative
inspirations its symbols generate.

Alchemical images depict an intermediate realm, which is neither physical nor spiritual but which includes something of each. As Nathan
Schwartz-Salant pointed out, alchemy is about the in-between states.[4] His
understanding of the in-between states takes him to the realm of field theory. There are some quite useful concepts to be found in this theory, but my
primary concern is studying the in-between state itself—the psychoid
realm. Alchemy is indeed about the in-between state, for its operations cannot succeed if they are unable to combine both spirit and matter. The
alchemists were aware that to effect transformation, spirit needed to
become matter, and matter needed to become spirit. Moreover, they sought
to invoke and apply spiritual powers and agencies when working with their
substances. By studying the alchemical conceptualization of these powers as
well as the nature of the *prima materia*, we can learn much about the psychoid world.

By the same token, we can discover in the alchemical writings the characteristics of psychoidal entities and the ways in which we might interact
with them. It is my assertion that the interaction between humans and psychoidal entities constitutes a process of mutual transformation and is the
basis of psychoidal alchemy. The key to this alchemy is a relationship
between the human and the psychoid and, as we shall see, this relationship
can be quite complex.

It has been normal for students of inner alchemy, that is, for those
who focus on alchemy as a process of the transformation of the soul, to
interpret symbols and processes as occurring within the psyche of the
alchemist himself. I have done this myself in my earlier work, and it is a
useful approach for highlighting and explaining the processes by which
human beings may create the Self, the inner psychic center. However, I
also emphasized that the creation of the Self was not the end of alchemical work. Once the Self has begun to manifest, the individual may turn to
the transpsychic world and seek to create a union with it. The means by
which this union is accomplished is the interaction with the center of the
divine world that I have called "the ally." The ally is a psychoidal figure
through which the divinity incarnates, and by relating to the ally, the
human being creates a union with the incarnating divinity. Once the inner
psychic self has united with the divine through the agency of the ally, the
Philosopher's Stone comes into being. The ally is the power that unites the

opposites of human and divine, which gives birth to the Stone, but the ally is the Stone itself, as well.

There are other psychoidal entities besides the ally, however, that play a role in alchemy, such as Sophia. There are also many models for understanding how the Stone comes into being. All of these concern the union of opposites. In the first model presented in my first book, the opposites were the divinity and the human being. Here, I am considering the opposites of the feminine and masculine aspects of God. The ally is once more the end product of this union. Though the text of the *Aurora* does discuss the child of the union of Sophia and the king, or God, and the illustrations that accompany this text show Sophia giving birth, my concern in this book is not with the ally or God, but with Sophia and her role in the alchemical process.

Sophia, or Divine Wisdom, is a crucial figure in many of the alchemical writings. Furthermore, there is a great deal of literature about Sophia that will help to explain her nature and characteristics insofar as they can be captured by human thought. In chapter 2 I shall make use of some of these non-alchemical writings to set the stage for understanding Sophia in the alchemical context. In addition, I shall present some of the main alchemical writings about Sophia. Having created at least an image of who Sophia is, I shall go on to illustrate psychoidal alchemy as it is presented in the *Aurora Consurgens*.

There was another consideration in my choice of writing about Sophia, and that is the current interest in her, which stems not only from the feminist movement and from those who seek to know her as a goddess, but also from those concerned with the reemergence of the feminine principal. It is not my intention to rehabilitate Sophia as a goddess because I am not, nor do I believe she is, interested in worship. Rather, psychoidal alchemy seeks to create a relationship with Sophia that transforms both the human being and Sophia herself.

The alchemists speak of the Philosopher's Stone as a living being that possesses many aspects in common with the ally. The Stone is unique, unites the higher and lower worlds within itself, has magical power over creative processes, and is involved in a love relationship with the alchemist. All of these characteristics are true of the ally as well.

Although Sophia and God are two halves becoming one in the ally, Sophia does not disappear as an individual being, but she is simultaneously part of the ally. As one with the ally, Sophia ceases to be a collective goddess and becomes unique and individualized. Therefore, rather than creating a new collective image of the feminine, psychoidal alchemy personalizes the experience of that image.

Having presented Sophia as a psychoidal figure, I devote the remaining chapters to my analysis of the *Aurora Consurgens*. It is my theory that this book portrays the experience of an individual alchemist and his encounter with Sophia. Through the profound and numinous experience depicted in this work, we glimpse the nature of both psychoidal experience and psychoidal alchemy, for the text ends with the mystical union of Sophia with the king. It is one of the best texts for understanding the profound transformation experienced in psychoidal alchemy. As von Franz has demonstrated, the author of the *Aurora* clearly underwent some profound spiritual experience. The text is an ecstatic presentation of his experience, and is in many ways unique among alchemical writings. It does not simply repeat the alchemical formulas found in almost every alchemical work, but communicates a very personal, intimate experience that the author understood in alchemical terms. I believe that he gave expression to his experience using alchemical imagery not simply (as von Franz maintained) because alchemy compensated a one-sided Christian attitude, but because his experience was by its very nature alchemical. If we can understand his experience we will gain deeper insights into the nature of alchemy itself.

There are many examples of ecstatic expression in the literature of alchemy. The ecstasy of the alchemists cannot be explained by a purely material conception of their work but indicates the numinous experiences that are generic to alchemy itself. Nor must we explain away these experiences as an invasion of the unconscious, for that does an injustice to the wisdom of the alchemists. We shall discover by a close examination of the experiences of the author of the *Aurora* that the ecstatic nature of the alchemical adventure had much to do with its encounter of the psychoid and of the figures that emerge from it.

As I mentioned at the beginning, we may take many perspectives when dealing with alchemical material. I cannot, of course, maintain that all alchemists were dealing with the psychoid, but I do maintain that many of them were, and that the psychoidal element permeates much of alchemical literature. I have discovered in my own research that adding the concept of the psychoid to our understanding of alchemy leads to many insights and a deeper appreciation of alchemy as a spiritual tradition. Many writers have criticized Jung for taking the position that the alchemists projected the unconscious onto the mystery of matter. Though often such criticism is based on misunderstanding, there is some truth to it. I do not deny the importance of the conscious attempt on the part of the alchemists to perform a very special transmutation and to engender a spiritual experience. This is not to say that the alchemists always knew what they were about, for there is clear evidence that many were groping in the dark, creating symbols whose ultimate meaning they did not understand. I have attempted to appreciate both the tradition that the alchemists were consciously following and interpret the symbols that they created from my own perspective. My interpretation is therefore rooted in alchemy but reflects my own experience and inner understanding.

From its beginning, much of alchemy was based in *gnosis*; direct and immediate perception of reality. By the same token, any good interpretation must be based in gnosis. I have always attempted to balance my own inner understanding with respect for the outer alchemical tradition. I therefore do not believe that the alchemists were simply projecting, for to take such a view dismisses the great tradition of alchemy as a mystery religion. But I also do not assume that the alchemists were always correct in the interpretation of their own experience. I have combined the interpretation of the alchemical symbols with my own experience of gnosis. I do not write of the Sophia only as I have experienced her in the alchemical literature, but as I have known her through the Gnostic imagination as well.

In order to root myself in the alchemical tradition, I shall use alchemical texts whenever possible to illustrate and amplify the ideas I am trying to convey but, by the very nature of things, I shall interpret these texts according to my own lens. I accept full responsibility for any bias I may bring to this work, but I also recognize the impossibility of ignoring one's own point of view. It is not possible to avoid such bias, and it is essential to acknowledge it and to allow for other points of view.

Many years ago, I began to have experiences that convinced me that there was a realm beyond the human psyche in which spiritual forces and energies manifested. I turned to the study of earlier traditions as much to understand my own experiences as to appreciate those traditions. In many of the traditions that I studied, such as Gnosticism, shamanism, Sufism, Kabbalah, and alchemy, I discovered concepts dealing with an intermediate realm that lay between the highest heavens and the world of ordinary reality. I was fascinated by this intermediate realm and by the implications of its existence for understanding both ordinary life as well as spiritual experience. I was also captivated by the notion of the imagination that many of these traditions portrayed. We cannot understand alchemy or the psychoid realm without understanding the role of imagination. I tried in my earlier book to discuss the alchemical imagination and to demonstrate its value and importance to the individuation process. In this book, I will focus on the role of imagination in psychoidal experience, and not on its part in the process of individuation.

My understanding of psychoidal alchemy assumes that those performing it have traveled far on the road to individuation. Just as many of the alchemists assumed that those who were studying their work were already well-developed in personal ethics and moral responsibility, I realize that the understanding and experience of psychoidal alchemy requires a relationship with the unconscious and a good deal of self-knowledge and self-awareness. I do not expect you to have individuated, but I caution you nonetheless that experience engenders understanding, and that much of what I discuss can only truly be comprehended by direct experience. On the other hand, just as experience engenders understanding, so too may understanding create experience. It is my hope that this book will produce an understanding of the intermediate realm I call the psychoid and of the reality of the spirits that manifest within it. If you come to understand the existence of this realm and the reality of the experiences you may have within it, you will be more likely to have such experiences. This is important, for we live in a world in which we are not only split from ourselves, but also from the spiritual world that could nourish and enrich our lives. Wholeness, healing, and harmony in human life require not only self-knowledge but also knowledge of the Other; in fact, it requires not only knowledge of the Other but also relationship to it. This relationship is discovered in and through the imagination.

When reading this material, keep in mind that I use the terms "masculine" and "feminine" to describe the opposite sides of God. In this text, "God" means the divine, in all of its manifestations. Sophia represents the so-called feminine side of God. Unfortunately, the English language is extremely limited in its descriptive terms for gender. "Masculine" and "feminine" are two words with which we are expected to describe myriad qualities that have nothing to do with gender per se, but are more about how the psyche and soul of the individual relate to the world. Unlike the Inuit who have many words for snow, or the people in India who have many terms for love, we are limited by the terms masculine and feminine to describe these seemingly infinite energies. Therefore, the alchemist's description of his "marriage" to Sophia, and Sophia's union with the "masculine" side of God need to be interpreted with this in mind; that we are speaking about energies that have masculine and feminine qualities.

The alchemist/individual involved in psychoidal alchemy is just that; an individual, regardless of gender, race, or sexual orientation. Remember that terms such as masculine, feminine, *anima, filius,* and marriage are simply symbols and words for concepts that are much larger than our vocabulary. This book is about imagination. It asks you to use your imagination to contain these ideas, and to avoid the pitfall of limiting these concepts to gender, sexuality, and literal-mindedness.

CHAPTER 1

IMAGINAL REALITIES AND IMAGINATION

The great Sufi master, Ibn Arabi, had a high opinion of the human being, who was made in the image of God. He declared that the human being is noble, for in him or her "God made the locus of the spiritualities of [all of] these entities! For God originated his 'image' when He caused him to become His Most-Perfect Transcription."[1] This exalted view of the human being is inherent in the esoteric tradition. The Gnostics and alchemists, as well as the Sufis, contend that humankind holds a remarkable place in the universe and is higher than the angels. In the *Corpus Hermeticum*, the basis of much of hermetic thought, Poimandres tells Tat that you cannot understand God unless "you make yourself equal to god . . . Make yourself grow to immeasurable immensity, outleap all body, outstrip all time, become eternity and you will become god."[2] We are higher than even the angels because, through our mind, which is something like our self or our imagination, we can become even as God. The human being thus has the innate capacity to unite with the higher world, and to unite the higher and the lower worlds as one.

But along with humans and angels, there are other psychoidal forces in the universe—demons and archons. In the *Corpus Hermeticum*, Asclepius warns that

> [T]he sun sets in array the troop, or rather troops, of demons, which are many and changing, arrayed under the regiments of stars, an equal number of them for each star. Thus deployed, they follow the orders of a particular star, and they are good and evil according to their natures—their energies, that is. For energy is the essence of a demon . . . They have all been granted authority over

the things of the earth and over the troubles of the earth, and they produce change and tumult, collectively for cities and nations, individually for each person. They reshape our souls to their own ends, and they rouse them, lying in ambush in our muscle and marrow, in veins and arteries, in the brain itself, reaching to the very guts.[3]

The strange paradox that humans are considered god-like and are yet the slaves of demons is also part of the esoteric tradition. There are psychoidal forces and entities that control us, unless we release the potential found within ourselves to control them and prevent them from dominating us. The struggle for freedom and divinity, and the need to order the forces of the psychoid is described in alchemy, for the Philosopher's Stone starts out in a chaotic condition dominated by the other forces of the universe. However, through the alchemist's effort, it gains the strength to bring order to the psychoid world and escapes the dominion of the forces that inhabit it.

In Sufi and Kabbalistic speculation, the psychoidal aspects of God that counterbalance the dominating psychoidal forces are termed "Names." A Name is not just a word or a title, it is a living being that has its own life, while expressing and personifying some particular aspect of God. Ibn Arabi explains, "No one can know the true essence of god but even the greatest stop at the final veil for the essence shines forth in the Names and attributes."[4] In other words, neither the godhead nor the worlds of pure spirit are perceptible. We would not know God unless God revealed Itself through the manifestation of Names.

A Name might be something like Compassion, Immensity, or Wisdom. Ibn Arabi calls the human being the locus of spirituality for, as the image of God, the human soul contains all the Names. There are therefore Names within God that manifest, and Names within the human being that can be known and expressed. Yet even though Names belong to both soul and divinity, they are of a different order in each. Wisdom is a feminine Name of God, and we can know Her within ourselves as a feminine archetype that teaches and guides. But the wisdom that a human being possesses can in no way compare to the Wisdom that emerges from the godhead. Thus, when the Name of Wisdom appears it is recognizable because of the archetype of wisdom, but it reveals itself as a divine force that we can only recognize with awe. Though the human psyche does not possess this same order of wisdom, it can relate to the Name Wisdom and receive Her revelations and teachings.

Thus, there are Names that belong to the psyche and Names that belong to the psychoid. Names within the psyche are archetypes, which are universal images and ways of perceiving reality found in each of us.

According the Sufi theorists, and in my own experiences as well, there are two opposite worlds: the material world and the world of pure spirit or Idea. Acting as an intermediary between these worlds is a "third world" of imagination, the psychoid world. A spirit or a Name originates from the world of pure spirit where it has a life unknowable to the human mind. Through a series of processes, this spirit crosses a threshold and makes itself known to us as a psychoidal being. The Zohar (the "bible" of the Kabbalistic tradition) states, "whenever the celestial spirits descend to earth, they clothe themselves in corporeal elements and appear to men in human shape."[5] A psychoidal being is in its essence spiritual, yet it assumes a subtle body that has both spirit and a degree of corporality. We can say that the essence or soul of the psychoidal being and its form are one and the same. The phenomenon of light holds the closest analogy to a psychoidal being. Light is both matter, or particles, and energy, or waves. It cannot be restricted to one manifestation or another. The psychoidal entity is neither matter nor spirit, but both at the same time. A human being possess a soul encased within a body and though the two are very much interrelated they are still separate. Only the human being who has experienced the subtle body understands the nature of the psychoidal "matter" and its interaction with "spirit." In the psychoid, consciousness and body are one.

There is a field of energy, or vibration, a zone of manifestation that appears in between the spiritual and mundane worlds. This energy, for lack of a better word, is formless and corresponds to the alchemical *prima materia*. Yet, it is plastic, and when a Name enters the imaginative realm, it first molds the energy into a form. This form is substantial, having something of the material about it, but subtle, retaining something of the spiritual as well. It appears as a light/energy shape but has not yet taken on the form of an image. Every psychoidal entity has a certain vibratory quality and often appears as an energy form that we may see or feel, but which has no defining imaginal characteristic to it. Some psychoidal experiences are of these forms only, but others engage the imagination more specifically.

The next stage of the entity's manifestation in the psychoid imagination is for it to assume some more defined imaginal form. For example, in my experience of Sophia, she appeared as a vibratory presence that I could see and feel in the room, but at the same time, emanating from her was the image of the most beautiful woman I had ever seen. There was no doubt that she was a goddess of great compassion, love, and wisdom. I saw and felt both her image and her vibration simultaneously.

In my experience and that of my clients, the Name, as it crosses into the psychoid, molds the vibratory energy around itself to assume an image that is expressive of its own nature while appealing to the imagery most familiar to the human being to whom it is manifesting. A Christian might see a Name as Jesus, while a Sufi might see the same Name as Mohammad, and a Buddhist, as Buddha. Behind each of these images is the same Name, which exists as a psychoidal being, and which puts on the image it has chosen as if it were putting on clothes. Names choose their clothes well, in order to communicate something of themselves to the individual to whom they are appearing, even before any words are spoken. But after working with them for some time, an individual may come to perceive them without any such imaginal clothing, simply as a particular vibratory energy that the individual recognizes by its feel and essence. One of the major differences between a psychological imaginative experience and a psychoidal one is the energetic and vibrational quality of the psychoid entity.

In summary, there exists an original Idea, Name, or Aspect of God that wishes to manifest in order to be known. A particular Name enters an energy field that is the *prima materia* of the psychoid and creates a form or body made from this energy field, and then manifests itself and its teaching by generating an image, that is, by imagining. When an individual experiences this imagination, he or she comes to know that Name.

The Name not only personifies itself in an image, but also may teach, or create a variety of imaginal experiences. It can create a visual expression of itself, as well as dialogue with a person, or even create whole scenes and even worlds based on its essential nature. That is why Ibn Arabi spoke of the Name as having its own world. Through the imagination, it can lift an individual into its own reality, which at the same time is an aspect of the reality of God. Because these experiences partake of the psychoidal imagination, they are perceived as being completely real.

The human being who attains his or her wholeness, or Self in the image of God, orders the archetypes around a common center. When he or she wishes to encounter the divinity, these same archetypes are met as Names in the psychoid. The human being meets these beings in the imagination, in the imaginal world that connects one to the place of pure spirit. The godhead manifests as a seemingly vast number of Names, each of which is alive. Not only that, but each human being has a particular Name of his or her own. Ibn Arabi says that God, though one in essence, is "All through the names. No existent thing has anything from God except its own specific Lord. It cannot possibly have the All. . . . That which becomes designated for it from the All is only that which corresponds to it, and that is its own Lord." Every Name is a living manifestation of the All and expresses God for its lover. Thus, each Name is its own image of reality and of God and normally embodies a particular way to relate to that image of God. We all have our own God which is unique to us.[6]

The Names that exist within the human being as archetypes exist in the godhead as pure spirit and are unknowable until they manifest as psychoidal beings, each in their own place and in their own world. If the human being comes face to face with God, both reveal these Names. In a somewhat complicated statement, Ibn Arabi says that, "All that I will show to you, which the Merciful has deposited [also] in your Essence and placed among the sum of your attributes. For you are the 'Anthropomorphic Image' [of God] and *That* is the [Divine] 'Transcendent Image.' If you ask, 'But what do *I* have to do with "Anthropomorphism"?' [I tell you that] with the 'Bringing face-to-Face' and the 'Raising to Preeminence', both of You [*viz.* both God and you] oscillate between Transcendence and Anthropomorphism."[7] In other words, we can glimpse the transcendent nature of the godhead and possess something of its transcendent nature, while the godhead is also never completely transcendent but appears in anthropomorphic Names, which appear as living Images. In this sense, the Names unite the transcendent and the immanent, the impersonal and the anthropomorphic.

Face to face, the archetypes within the psyche match the Names of God, and so we can first experience them as inner psychic figures, but eventually we must experience them as objective psychoidal beings. Both are necessary; both the archetypes and the Names must be harmonized so that total union between the human being and God may occur. Sometimes we work with the archetypes, sometimes with the Names, and sometimes with both, but if we did not possess the inner Names we could not resonate with the outer Names, nor would we be the image of God.

Many times when we are doing active imagination we are not touching the psychoid, but inner figures. Yet as these inner figures are the reflection of the Names, it doesn't matter so much at the beginning, because knowing the archetypes is first necessary to familiarize ourselves with the nature of the Name. To experience an archetype that is rooted in the psychoidal Name is to experience something of great power, but to experience the Name is to encounter power far exceeding that of the archetype. We

must be ready for such an experience, and the best way to prepare is to
know the archetype.

Let us once more use the example of Sophia who, for the Sufi, Jewish,
and Christian traditions is the feminine Name of Divine Wisdom. We can
experience Sophia as an archetype, in the form of a man's anima or a
woman's self-figure. This allows us to experience a feminine power within
the psyche, which forms part of the self, and contributes greatly to our
individual wholeness. She can act as a guide and teach us about the creative
powers of the self, but she has as her correlate an extra psychic or psychoidal living being, a feminine goddess who forms the Name Wisdom.
When we encounter her as a Name, we are experiencing a being born in the
depths of the godhead. It is an amazingly powerful experience. She teaches
us about the nature of the divine reality, about our place in the universe,
and other mysteries. When we contact her, we do not experience an inner
image, but a vibrational energy and an image of a woman whose numinosity can bring us chills. We feel her outside ourselves and communicate
in a way that is difficult to intellectualize. By first knowing the archetype
we are more prepared to experience the living Name, and, in fact, by relating to the archetype we open the door for the Name to come through.

IMAGINATION

When Ibn Arabi referred to the human as the locus of spirituality, he was also
addressing the time in our individual development when we must come
face-to-face with God. When this occurs, we experience our own inner
Names, as well as the anthropomorphism of God, or the manifestation of Its
Names. We come face to face with the living Realities that power our archetypal inner figures. How do we do this? We do it through the imagination.

Imagination is critical in understanding the alchemical *opus* as well as
experiencing the process of individuation. But imagination is still deni-
grated in our society, and even when it is not, it is little understood. I am in
touch with several individuals who are engaged in the study of imagination,
attempting to come to a contemporary formulation of this wonderful fac-
ulty. There are many questions still unanswered in our attempt to express
some consistent theory of imagination, but I am prepared to offer some initial ideas.

The first step is to differentiate the diverse levels, or *loci*, of the imagination. To begin with, we must be able to distinguish fantasy from true

imagination. Fantasy serves the purposes of the ego. The ego fantasizes about its achievements, power, beauty, or sexual exploits, but whatever the fantasy it serves to create a pleasing sensation and image of the ego. This can include negative fantasy, for there are many individuals who are hooked on fantasizing about how terrible they are and what horrible mistakes they have made. They can indulge in this fantasy for hours, deriving some reassurance from "knowing" just how dreadful they are. In either the positive or negative cases, however, the point of the exercise is to create a story or an image in which the ego is the star.

The mystic Jacob Boehme and the alchemist Paracelsus offer us further information about fantasy, arguing that it is a misperception of reality.[8] According to Boehme, fantasies were delusions that led one away from God. Lucifer indulged in fantasies of power and dominance, and even imagined rivaling God. Instead of imagining about God, he imagined about himself being God. Adam was led astray by his false imagings, which carried him into the world of senses instead of remaining in paradise with God.

According to Paracelsus, fantasy is seeing only the surface of things. It fails to penetrate the veils of nature and spirit to see into the heart of something, and is content with superficialities. Fantasy can be creative, as a scientist can be creative about the nature of physical reality, but if such a scientist fails to understand the natural object as a symbol, and to perceive the meaning of that symbol, he has engaged in fantasy and not in true imagination. Boehme's concept of fantasy emphasizes the ego's delusion about its own nature, as with Lucifer and Adam. For Paracelsus, fantasy is the failure to recognize a symbol and the symbolic reality of all things.

The Four Attributes of Psychological Imagination

With Paracelsus we come to the first of four attributes of the imagination. The first attribute of the imagination is that it teaches by conveying information through the creation of a symbol. To understand this function, we must keep in mind that the ego does not control the imagination nor produce it. The spiritual power of the Self creates images. The ego experiences these images and can interact with them in active imagination, but it does not create them. According to the Sufis, the soul receives the influx of the Active Intelligence of God, who creates the imaginal experience.

There are both intrapsychic and psychoidal imaginal experiences. In both types, there occurs the spontaneous creation of a symbol that may appear in a dream, or in active imagination. The symbol may not be the personification of an inner figure, but often is the imaginal depiction of ideas, feelings, or insights. Poetry is the symbolic expression of feeling and insight, for example, and true poetry arises from the imagination. When a poet uses a symbol, he or she attempts to bring some insight to life in the form of an image or word picture. Dreams, as well, can be poetic by presenting symbols that teach us about life. One of my clients had a dream of monstrous parents devouring their own children, and experienced in this dream all the horrors felt by the children as their parents betrayed them. The dream image created a feeling and an insight into the darker side of life where parents hurt their own children.

The imagination thus conveys information about life, about the ego and its problems, and about God and the nature of reality by creating symbols that teach through the feelings and insights they produce. The first function of the imagination is very common since everyone has experienced it either through their dreams or their experience of imaginative literature.

The second function of the psychological imagination is personification. As I state in my earlier book, anything within the psyche may personify, whether it is an affect, a complex, or an archetype. The personifications create inner figures that come alive within the imaginal experience to engage the ego in dialogue or activity of some kind. For example, I may dream of my father, mother, wife, or some unknown figure who performs certain behavior to which I must respond. The figure within the dream is the personification of some content of the unconscious. These figures are alive and have their own autonomy. They act, do, and say what they choose, and I can only respond as seems best to me. The autonomy of the inner figure and its capacity to speak and act on its own is the basis of active imagination and much of the work of individuation, which consists of coming to terms with these figures and, through interaction with them, integrating them into the manifest Self.

Third, the imagination has a power that I call activation. This corresponds with the well-known fact that when the ego pays attention to it, a content of the unconscious becomes activated and soon manifests in dream or active imagination. If I begin to reflect on an issue, conflict, or inner figure, that content usually appears within the imagination. As long as I continue the process of imagining with it, it continues to appear. For example, if I do an active imagination with an inner figure I am likely to dream either about that inner figure or the issue we discussed. Alternatively, if I dream about an inner figure, it is likely to appear in my active imagination. There can develop an on-going process of dream leading to active imagination

leading to dream. Activation can also occur when, for example, I spontaneously dream about a topic I was not previously interested in, but after the
dream find my interest intensified.

Finally, the imagination has the capacity to transform. What we dream
is now happening or will soon happen within the psyche. The activity of the
dream depicts movement and transformation within the psyche, and for
this reason Jung called images "symbols of transformation." Dreams produce their own kind of transformation within the psyche, but when the ego
becomes more consciously involved either in interpretation or in active
imagination, the degree of transformation is greater. Learning from and
applying the messages of our imaginal experience creates changes in attitude, behavior, and even states of consciousness. Moreover, the imagination
creates what Jung termed the "transcendent function," through which profound changes within the Self occurs, and by which the manifest Self is generated. Through imagination, transformation occurs and the Self is born.
Thus, imagination is the central force in the process of individuation or the
attainment of psychological wholeness.

Gnostic Imagination

The Gnostic imagination is even more profound in its impact than the psychological imagination. This is because the source of the imaginal experience is from the psychoid, and often from very powerful psychoidal entities.
Moreover, the very nature of psychoidal imaginal experiences creates a
deeper sense of reality. For example, in an active imagination I may imagine
that a teaching figure comes into my room and touches me on the chest
producing a feeling of ecstasy. For this to be a genuine active I should
feel/see the inner figure walk in, feel his touch, and feel some measure of
ecstatic reaction. But all of this is happening in my mind's eye. In psychoidal
imagination, an inner figure actually does walk into my room, and when he
touches me it feels like a genuine physical touch and I go into an altered
state of ecstatic nature. The figure is not present in a wholly physical way,
but there is a physical component to the experience that makes it quite different from a purely inner one. Not only does the experience feel different,
I perceive it in an entirely different fashion. I may find myself in another
landscape, or in the presence of strange beings, or in a profoundly altered
state in which I gain wisdom or have intense visions. The Gnostic imagination takes place in a world of its own that cannot be located within the psyche. The Gnostic imagination ultimately belongs to the divine, though we

may have psychoidal experiences of lesser beings who have their own powers of imagination that allow them to manifest in different types of experiences, such as ghost or poltergeists. For the seeker, the Gnostic imagination is about the divine power and nature touching us.

According to Ibn Arabi, everything that is not God is imagined by God, and so comes into existence. In this sense, everything in the cosmos is a symbol of an aspect of the divinity. This is the symbolic nature of reality to which Paracelsus referred when he said that true imagination perceives the underlying essence of things. For the Sufi, as well as the alchemist, the underlying essence is divine, and so we can learn about God from the book of life, or what the alchemists call the book of nature. Everything that is and everything that happens is a symbolic expression of the imagination of the divine, and if we interpret that symbol correctly or interact with it appropriately, we are in touch with the divine. Thus everywhere we look, if we look deeply, we find the symbolic expression of the Gnostic imagination.

Names

Just as the imagination of the Self personifies the contents of the unconscious, so do psychoidal figures personify the divine imagination. These psychoidal beings exist in their own right, and we may interact with them. The Sufis speak of jinn, or angels, who are created beings, like ourselves, who require our deep imaginal experience to be brought into our consciousness. Just as an archetype may personify itself in the psyche and communicate with the ego, so an angel may appear as an imaginal figure and communicate with the human being. But of highest significance are the Names of God, those personified psychoidal figures that are aspects of the One Thing, alive in their own right, with their own awareness and consciousness. Ibn Arabi even suggests that they are not aware of each other, except for the highest of the Names. He says that they each possess their own truth, law, and way and he suggests elsewhere that they create their own world as well.[9] Wisdom, as a divine Name of God, personifies as a feminine being and possesses knowledge about the other divine Names, the nature of reality, and the nature of the human being, and communicates this to us in imaginal encounters. But we perceive her as a living being of intense beauty, warmth, and numinosity. As long as we work with her and accept her as our Name, we would live with her and follow her ways. It would seem as if we lived in her world. Thus, many who experienced Sophia as the Name of God spoke of divine marriage with her, of looking forward to the afterlife where they would join her in paradise, and so on. Jacob Boehme, for example, says that if he holds to the Christ well enough He will bring his soul to Sophia in Paradise: "I will give the venture, and go through the Thistles and Thorns, as well as I can, till I find my native country again, out of which my soul is wandered, where my dearest Virgin dwells." He goes on to report an encounter that he had with her:

> I rely upon her faithful, when she appeared to me, but she turned all my Mournings into Joy; and when I laid upon the Mountains toward the North, so that all the Tress fell upon me, and all the Storms and Winds beat upon me, and Antichrist gave at me with his open jaws to devour me, and she came and comforted me, and married her self to me." 10

For Boehme, Sophia was an aspect of the divine to whom he committed himself in the mystical marriage and to whom he longed to rejoin in heaven; such is the power and spiritual impact of a Name of God when it appears to an individual.

Psychoidal figures possess the same ability as inner figures to activate and transform, yet in greater measure. They may come with a message to change our life or to undertake some work, or they may teach us something of the divine nature. Since I have within myself all the archetypes that correspond to the divine Names, the visitation of the Name will activate that archetype and force me to pay attention to and work with it. A visitation from Sophia, for example, will activate the anima, and invite and sometimes force me to deal with my feminine nature. It will stimulate me as well in the pursuit of wisdom, which may take the form of study or increased work in active imagination. But whatever the Name that comes, and whatever the message, it stimulates the psyche into intense activity.

The Names are also transformative in their impact. Their capacity to transform is truly amazing and takes us to a fact noted by mystics of all religions: The voice that emerges from God or a divine personification of God has the power not only to speak a word, but to create what the word denotes. According to Islam, Judaism, and Christianity, as well as some traditions in Hinduism, God created the universe through speech. What God says comes to be. The words spoken by the Name therefore impact the person profoundly, and may create transformation directly as they are spoken. I have witnessed psychoidal figures heal physical ailments, create altered states of consciousness by their touch or their word, and cause more psychological transformation in a five-minute encounter than might occur in a year.

Transformation is not always created by speech, but can occur through any contact with the Names. The Gnostic imagination is capable of producing an infinite variety of experiences, each of which is powerful and transformative. The ultimate goal of the operations of the Gnostic imagination is to manifest the godhead, for without the imaginal form it would remain hidden and unknowable. The Gnostic imagines in order to know God in all of its many aspects.

Knowing, however, has a power of its own. I mentioned earlier that an aspect of the imagination is transformation, and transformation is the core process of alchemy. Alchemy does not simply seek to know things, but to transform them as well. Another alchemical motif is redemption, and often in alchemical writings the transformation and redemption are portrayed as occurring within something other than the human being. If we add alchemical transformation and redemption to the ideas of the imagination we have been discussing, we can see that the human being who encounters a Name through the Gnostic imagination has the capacity to transform that Name as well as be transformed by it. Though this is not a major motif among the Sufis, as far as I know, it finds reflections in the Kabbalistic view of the divinity. Though in and of itself, the godhead, known as *En Sof*, remains perfect and unknowable, it manifests its attributes through Names just as in the Sufi system. It emanates itself in the Kabbalistic tree through the ten Sephiroth. But in most systems of the Kabbalah there has entered into creation an imbalance in the tree, so that the various Sephiroth are out of balance with each other, and evil results follow. Through prayer and meditation, the Kabbalist has an impact on the manifest divine forces and can bring them back into balance. This is usually depicted as a sacred marriage between Malkhut (judgment) and Tifereth (mercy), the feminine and masculine principles. In any event, the intervention of the Kabbalist has direct impact on the manifestation of God and the order of the universe.

The same ideas apply in psychoidal alchemy. Psychoidal alchemy is the imaginative encounter between human consciousness and a psychoidal being, a Name of God. In the course of this encounter, one or both of the participants are transformed in some way. As we shall see in the *Aurora Consurgens*, the entity Sophia portrays herself as wounded and in need of help. She is healed through the alchemical operations presented in the text, all of which relate to imaginative experiences that unfold between her and the alchemist. Moreover, in the text, the alchemist sometimes finds himself replaced by another psychoidal being, as the masculine and feminine are united in the forms of Sophia and a God-image. The *coniunctio* that occurs, while witnessed by the alchemist, occurs through the interaction of the two psychoidal figures. The alchemical operations leading to the *coniunctio* all take place in the Gnostic imagination.

It is important, then, to add to the Sufi concept of the imagination the fact that the Names of God, through their interaction with a human being, undergo transformation. The Names are not perfect, and require human assistance to find their appropriate place in the scheme of things. The Kabbalist often defines evil as things being out of place, and the Kabbalist him- or herself must work to put things in their proper place. Sometimes this is done through prayer and following the commandments, but sometimes balance is accomplished through esoteric knowledge and meditation. Like the Kabbalah, psychoidal alchemy is the process of restoring things to their proper place and brings healing to the psychoidal entities. The alchemist witnesses and participates in the transformation. All depends on the imagination.

·   ·   ·

Imagination is the crucial element in the process of individuation. It is the means by which the conscious and the unconscious come into union, thereby manifesting the Self. Imagination of a different order, psychoidal imagination, is the means by which we encounter the Names or attributes of the infinite. It is through imagination that we transform the Names and experience our own transformation. The *Aurora Consurgens* is the depiction of the imaginal work that occurs when the alchemist encounters the Name Sophia, or Wisdom. In order to understand the nature of the experience, it is necessary to understand Sophia, so we shall now turn to a discussion of Sophia as a psychoidal being, as a Name of God.

CHAPTER 2

THE NATURE OF SOPHIA

S ophia is a psychoidal being closely connected to the feminine side of the Godhead and is therefore a mystery that we can never fully understand. But by working with the symbols that describe her, considering the experiences that some people have had of her, and by meditating on her, we shall gain some impression of her nature. I will approach the task of presenting Sophia by speaking of several motifs that are found in connection with her in Gnosticism, the apocryphal *Wisdom of Solomon*, the teachings of Jacob Boehme, and finally the writings of the alchemists. I will not attempt a comprehensive review of all the traditions concerning Sophia since there are several good books presenting much of this material already. Rather, I shall focus on a few main themes in the Sophianic tradition that establish her as a Name and indicate something of her power and nature.

THE DIVINE SOPHIA

The first motif is that of Sophia as a divinity. The exact nature of her divinity, and of her relationship to God, varies according to each tradition, and is different during various periods of the same tradition. In some cases, she is a Goddess in her own right; in some she is a passive partner of God, and in others an active partner of God. In each case, however, she possesses divinity in some measure, whether borrowed or not.

Often associated with the motif of the divine Sophia is that of the fallen Sophia, and there is a distinction between the higher and lower Sophia. Though Sophia is divine she has an inferior aspect, which, for different reasons in different traditions, has fallen away into the lower world. I shall treat this motif together with that of the divine Sophia since they are often presented together in her mythology.

One of the earliest examples of the divine Sophia is the apocryphal text, *The Wisdom of Solomon*. In many ways, this text is the primary source of the *Aurora Consurgen's* view of Wisdom, and the author quotes it repeatedly. After praising Wisdom and promising to tell everything he knows of Her, the author writes:

> For in her is a spirit intelligent and holy,
> unique in its kind yet manifold, subtle,
> agile, lucid, unsullied. . . .
> [she is] all-powerful, all-surveying,
> and pervading all spirits,
> intelligent, pure and most subtle.
> For wisdom is more mobile than any motion,
> she pervades and permeates all things by reason of her pureness.
>
> She is an exhaltation from the power of God,
> a pure effluence from the glory of the Almighty. . . .
> she is an effulgence of everlasting light.[1]

She is in some way the partner of God as well, for she enjoys "intimacy with God, and the Master of All loved her . . . she is initiate in the knowledge of God, and chooser of his works . . . what is richer than Wisdom, maker of all things?"[2] Sophia arises from God as a pure effluence, and is able to penetrate and permeate all things, a symbol of her divinity. She is related to light and she actually decides for God what He shall do. She is not a goddess *per se*, but an emanation of God. Nevertheless, she possesses all the attributes of divinity and is portrayed as being independent of God. Most of the traditions concerned with Sophia present her as an independent being. As an independent being, whatever her role in any hierarchy, she exhibits the autonomy and separate nature that qualifies her as a psychoidal entity and as a Name.

In *The Wisdom of Solomon*, she is a spiritual being possessing such great wisdom that she is God's advisor. Moreover, she is a very active principle, described as being the cause of things. In many traditions, Sophia is passive, and is often God's advisor, and even the mirror by which he knows himself. In any case, she is the wisdom through which creation unfolds.

Sophia's Divinity in Gnosticism

In the few remaining writings of Simon Magus, and in the attacks made upon him by early church writers, we can see that Sophia plays a large part in his system. Simon was a very early Gnostic who appears in the New Testament (Acts 8:9–24) as the energy of the apostles. Sophia, though originally divine, has been attacked by archons, or hostile gods, and trapped in matter, where she has gone through many reincarnations. Simon considered himself a divine being as well, whose task it was to redeem Sophia from her imprisonment. According to Mead's account of Simon's life:

> He took round with him a certain Helen, a hired prostitute from the Phoenician city Tyre, after he had purchased her freedom, saying that she was the first conception [or Thought] of his Mind, the Mother of All, by whom in the beginning he conceived in his Mind the making of the Angels and Archangels. That this Thought, leaping forth from him, and knowing what was the will of her Father, descended to the lower regions and generated the Angels and Powers, by whom also he said this world was made. And after she had generated them, they detained her through envy, for they did not wish to be thought to be the progeny of any other. As for himself, he was entirely unknown by them; and it was his Thought that was made prisoner by the Powers and Angels that has been emanated by her. And she suffered every kind of indignity at their hands, to prevent her re-ascending to her Father, even to being imprisoned in the human body and transmigrating into other female bodies, as from one vessel into another.[3]

So, for Simon Magus, Helen was an incarnation of Sophia. Though she is the fallen Sophia, in her self she is sacred and an aspect of the divine:

> Epinoia [Sophia] is a Power of many names. She is called the Mother, or All-Mother, Mother of the Living or Shining Mother, the Celestial Eve; the Power Above; the Holy Spirit. . . . Again she is called She of the Left-hand, as opposed to the Christos, He of the Right-hand; the Man-woman; Prouneikos; Matrix; Paradise; Eden; Achamoth; the Virgin; Barbelo; Daughter of Light; Merciful Mother; Consort of the Masculine One; Revelant of the Perfect Mysteries; Perfect Mercy; Revelant of the Mysteries of the Whole Magnitude; Hidden Mother, She who knows the Mysteries of the

Elect; the Holy Dove, who has given birth to the two Twins;
Ennoia; and by many another name varying according to the ter-
minology of the different systems, but ever preserving the root idea
of the World-Soul in the Macrocosm and the Soul in Man.[4]

Though Sophia has fallen into human form and even become a harlot, in her
divine nature she is the consort of God, the revealer of mysteries, the Hidden
Mother and Daughter of Light, and is clearly related to the world-soul, the
intelligence that is to the world what the soul is to the body. These are all
aspects of her that we are familiar with from Gnosticism and alchemy.

The other Gnostic texts also treat Sophia with great respect, though
they also speak often of the fallen Sophia. In the Apocryphon of John,
Sophia is the first thought of the unknown and holy god and is the father-
mother of all:

And [his Ennoia performed a] deed and she came forth, [namely]
she who had [appeared] before him in [the shine of] his light.
This is the [first power which was] before all of them (and)
[which came] forth from his mind. . . . This is the first thought, his
image; she became the womb of everything, for it is she who is
prior to them all, the Mother-Father, the first man, the holy Spirit,
the thrice-male, the thrice-powerful, the thrice-named androgynous one, and the eternal aeon among the invisible ones, and the
first to come forth.[5]

Sophia is the first thought of God, so not quite his equal, yet she becomes
the womb of all things and even takes on androgynous qualities. One of
the most prevalent images of Sophia is that of the womb of all creation.
She is the Mother of all things, but she needs a partner who will father creation as well. In the Apocryphon of John, she creates the world without a
partner and thereby creates a monstrous god, who in turn creates our
world. Horrified at what she has done, Sophia appeals for help and a sav-
ior god, presumably a Christ-like figure, is created to help her save the
fallen world.

Sophia next appears to Eve and sends into Eve her own light so that
Eve may teach Adam and restore him to the vision of the true light and the
true god:

And he (Adam) saw the woman beside him. And in that moment
the luminous Epinoia appeared, and she lifted the veil which lay

over his mind. And he became sober from the drunkenness of darkness. And he recognized his counter-image, and he said, 'This is indeed bone of my bones and flesh of my flesh. . . ." And our sister Sophia (is) she who came down in innocence in order to rectify her deficiency. Therefore she was called Life, which is the mother of the living. Through the foreknowledge of the sovereignty and through her they have tasted the perfect Knowledge.[6]

Sophia thus is the redeemer of her own deficiency and the rectifier of her own mistake. She is the bringer of the light and true wisdom. In this passage we see another of her many roles—a guide for souls. She brings true wisdom to Adam and Eve, and in the Gnostic sense is related to the serpent that tries to awaken Eve to her own true nature. She restores them to wakefulness, as she can restore all souls to awareness of their own light being. But, as the bringer of light, she is subject to the attack of the archons who do not want her to reveal the truth, and in one variant is raped repeatedly by them and once more held prisoner as the fallen Sophia:

He made a plan with his authorities [the archons], which are his powers, and they committed together adultery with Sophia, and bitter fate was begotten through them, which is the last of the terrible bonds. . . . For from that fate came forth every sin and injustice and blasphemy, and the chain of forgetfulness and ignorance and every difficult command, and serious sins and great fears. And thus the whole creation was made blind, in order that they may not know God, who is above all of them. And because of the chain of forgetfulness, their sins were hidden.[7]

Thus, in some sense, Sophia is both the bringer of light who awakens the soul to its true nature and the source of its darkness and forgetfulness of the true god. In several tellings of this myth, her fall is inadvertent, and by her rape and imprisonment all evil is created. Clearly, for the Gnostics, the two aspects of Sophia—that of the lower and the higher—are well known and well developed.

Sophia's Place in the Alchemical Tradition

The mystical alchemist Henry Khunrath wrote that Sophia was the true Magnesia of the great world and, in fact, was the Holy Spirit and an emanation of the Holy Trinity. She was with God from the beginning, though apparently proceeding from His essence, and was the spirit that moved upon the waters in Genesis. She is in all things, "even in ye most inward & sacredest Virgin wombe and centre of the Earth, the misticall broodie Mother of the greate world."[8]

Once again, Sophia is the mother of all creation, and the soul of the world found in all beings, even at the center of the earth. She is the Holy Ghost and, though second to God, was with Him before creation. Even more radical than Khunrath's view is that of the great Swiss alchemist, Paracelsus. A little-known fact about Paracelsus is that not only did he write on alchemy and medicine, he also wrote a great deal about theology. These writings have been neglected—I'm not sure why. His vision of Sophia is very powerful and presents her as almost co-equal with the members of the Trinity. Andrew Weeks explains:

> [T]he intention here is clearly to establish a place in the divine family for a higher prototype of the Virgin Mary, a goddess with whom the Father generates the divine Son in heaven prior to the birth of Jesus as God and man in this world. . . . Mary and before her Eve have a prototype in a "celestial queen," an eternally pure being, both a person and not a person, she is necessary for generating the divine family but not one of the three persons of the family.[9]

Though we have here once again the confusion about just how divine Sophia really was, bear in mind that Paracelsus was already perilously close to heresy, and any stronger statement about Sophia's divine place would have been dangerous. Nevertheless, she is a goddess of tremendous power and purity, and is necessary for the unfoldment within the divinity itself. Moreover, she has a more sublime aspect as the female principal in creation, for she could create the labor Sophiae, defined as "the other Paradise of this world, in which no disease grows, no disease remains, no poisonous creature dwells or enters . . ."[10]

Paracelsus therefore believed that Sophia was the feminine aspect of the godhead, and in her manifestation, if she were allowed to express her nature completely, she would create Paradise on earth in which the four elements and all materials would reach their fullest expression. She fulfills her role as creator of paradise when she becomes an aspect of the Philosopher's Stone in the *Aurora Consurgens.*

SOPHIA AS A PSYCHIC CONTENT

According to Dr. von Franz, Sophia is the anima, and as the anima she represents the personification of the collective unconscious, at least in the psyche of a man. Von Franz's study of the *Aurora Consurgens* unfortunately does not explain Sophia in terms of the psychology of a woman, certainly because she is analyzing the author of the *Aurora*, who is a man. Nevertheless, this is a grave weakness when considering women's psychology, and works against theorizing Sophia as simply the anima. Psychologically, Sophia appears more as an image of the self for women, and I have noted her appearance in many dreams of women clients. She thus would symbolize the feminine side of the self and as a model for what an individuated woman might experience within herself.

For a woman alchemist, Sophia represents the Philosopher's Stone perhaps more clearly than for the male alchemist. Nevertheless, as I have stressed, though at the psychological level Sophia represents different things for men and women, especially in regards to their work with the self, as a psychoidal figure Sophia is a force or power that must not be related to specific gender, any more than may the *filius*, or Mercurius, or other alchemical images. Gender is a symbolic form chosen by a specific entity. Sophia appears as a feminine being, but she is a not a woman. Women, as much as men, may embrace her with love and ecstasy as a divine partner and lover.

Still, von Franz's whole commentary is a good example of how this material is worked on a psychic level. But how do we work with the image from the psychoidal point of view?

In my experience of Sophia in which she came to me, touched me, and spoke to me a great deal, she was a living being, a psychoidal entity, alive with an ineffable vitality and power. I did not, for a moment, consider her an aspect of my own psyche. We cannot interpret Sophia in such a way as to reduce her to something psychic, such as the anima. We cannot decrease her reality or separateness at all. We must approach her as if we were meeting a human being and attempting to describe the main characteristics of this human being. If I were trying to describe myself, I might talk about my attributes such as what I look like, what my talents are, and so forth. Such a description at least gives a vague idea of who I am, and this is how we must deal with Sophia. We cannot interpret her; we must try to understand her.

In some ways this makes the symbolic material we have so far contemplated too concrete, for we do not share the same mindset as the Gnostics, for example. We cannot say simply and literally that Sophia was trapped in the world and became a prostitute through a series of reincarnations. We must instead try to find the middle ground between reductive interpretation and one that is too literal. This is a difficult task, and, in many ways, a new one. We must ask ourselves: What did the Gnostics mean when they described Sophia as a prostitute? Without talking about the archetypal prostitute alone we must examine the symbol and determine what it says about a living figure of Sophia. A psychoidal interpretation steers a course between the extremes of literal and reductive interpretation. We could escape this dilemma by declaring Sophia a mystery who can only be described symbolically, but that is too easy a way out. She is certainly a mystery, but she is a mystery to whom certain attributes have been given, and through the examination of these attributes we can answer in part two essential questions: What is the psychoidal entity Sophia, and what is the experience we might expect if we encounter this psychoidal entity?

SOPHIA AS A PSYCHOIDAL ENTITY

According to the *Wisdom of Solomon*, she is a subtle and penetrating spirit moving easily, able to go through all things. Let us start with this image. It is quite remarkable that the ability to penetrate all things is one of the attributes of the Philosopher's Stone, for in this penetrating ability lies its capacity to transform. Penetration is often considered a masculine attribute, and it is interesting that Sophia possesses it. In *Aion*, Jung relates penetration to splitting and so to discrimination, "which is the essence of conscious realization."[11] Von Franz notes that in Egypt the person who has gone through the process of resurrection properly has gained two powers: the power to assume any shape and "to move about through anything in this material world, a kind of ghostlike being which could walk through closed doors and manifest in any desired form. That is the highest goal of life after death . . . and the alchemists connected this idea with their concept of the philosopher stone, that divine nucleus in man which is immortal and ubiquitous and able to penetrate any material object. It is an experience of something immortal lasting beyond physical death."[12]

Thus, the capacity for penetrating material objects connects Sophia to the Philosopher's Stone and to the body of immortality. This capacity not only marks her as a spirit but as a fundamentally powerful and important one, for she can enter not just the physical object but also the spirit of everything, without exception. We can interpret this divine attribute of Sophia as the ability to enter into and know all that exists. This subtle, penetrating capacity is joined with the image of the mist, for she is an "effluence from the glory of the Almighty." David Winston explains that this effluence relates to moist vapor.[13] In *The Wisdom of Solomon*, the mist is associated with purity, but there are several other meanings of mist.

According to the *Penguin Dictionary of Symbols*, mist is associated with the first moments of creation: "[m]ist is also a symbol of the mixture of air, water and fire which existed prior to the creation of solid matter . . . as it was before the six days creation and before all things were given their shape."[14]

Sophia, arising as the mist from God, is created before the world itself is created. She is the first emanation from God. However, the mist relates to the most important of alchemical images, the *prima materia*. One alchemist writes of the *prima materia:* "Form and spirit, or the soul of the world abstractly taken, are the *prima materia* of the world and the chaos before all form. The Spirit of the world, concretely taken, comprehends the soul of the world and the primal matter whereof it was formed."[15] Sophia accordingly is related not only to the Philosopher's Stone, but also to the *prima materia* from which the stone is created. Whatever Name we begin our work with will become an aspect of the Philosopher's Stone, or the Manifested God. If we begin our work with Sophia as the *prima materia*, we shall end it with her as part of the stone. Clearly, however, we can see alchemical parallels in the earliest mythological statements about her.

These two images, that of being able to penetrate and of being like the mist, reappear later in *The Wisdom of Solomon*, in her ability to enter "holy souls, and render them friends of God and prophets."[16] She thus serves as a guide and a redeemer, and as an aspect of this attribute she knows all things and can teach mysteries to those whom she loves. As Solomon describes her, "she knows the past and infers the future; she understands the intricacies of argument and the resolution of riddles, she foreknows signs and wonders and the outcome of critical seasons and times." Moreover, since she arose before the act of creation itself, she participates with God in creation of the universe. As Solomon says, "she is initiate in the knowledge of God, and chooser of his works."[17]

Sophia is therefore the divine entity that emerges from the godhead before creation itself and guides all beings, even God. Her ability to penetrate permits her to know everything. This is important because she can enter the souls of human beings and lead them to their right path in life. Sophia knows and understands the essence of all things and serves as a guide to those who discover her in their own souls. These two fundamental characteristics of Sophia, as Wisdom and as a guide, recur whenever the figure of Sophia appears. Hers is a special kind of knowing, a gnosis, that we must imagine transcends the human way of knowing. She does not know through the five senses or through the four functions that Jung outlined. She knows directly and perceives instantly into the heart and essence of all things—a direct perception of truth and actuality similar to what I call "the felt vision," but one developed far beyond what the human being is capable of. She can transmit this perception to a person who opens himself or herself to her.

There is a third characteristic Solomon alludes to: his deep love for her. This quality is almost always found in the experience of Sophia. An individual experiencing Sophia would encounter a figure who knew him or her intimately, who knew what his or her path was and how to best achieve his or her proper place in life. The individual would also experience a being with whom he or she felt a profound mutual love.

SOPHIA'S ROLE IN THE GNOSTIC DRAMA

Gnosticism speaks of a true, original God from whom many other gods emanate. In time, a separation from the true God occurs and a false god proclaims himself ruler of the universe. Often it is this false god who creates humankind and keeps humankind ignorant of the nature of the true God. The human being is asleep and must awaken to find salvation. The awakening occurs through gnosis, or direct experience of the truth. Those who awaken to the truth return to the true God, and those who do not remain the slaves of the archons and false gods. What is Sophia's role in this Gnostic drama?

As we have seen, she has many roles and it would perhaps be a mistake to try to make all the texts agree about these roles. But we may extract from the stories certain qualities of Sophia that can be amplified and used to help build our growing knowledge about this psychoidal figure.

The Image of the Fallen Sophia

To begin with, there is the image of Sophia as the fallen or lower Sophia. According to Simon's model, she was abducted and raped by the false gods and archons, and in other stories she is forced to commit adultery with these same forces that lead to the creation of evil. If she herself is not fallen, then her misdeed of creating without the cooperation of her spouse causes the fall. In the context of the fallen or lower Sophia, she is referred to as whore and harlot. When she herself is not trapped within the material world, her lower image is related to Eve, who in some fashion embodies Sophia. In one form or another, however, the Gnostic drama is about the separation from the true God, and Sophia either helps to create the separation or is a victim of it.

The Jungian school understands this motif as it relates to the process of individuation and the transformation of the psyche. The soul lost in matter corresponds to the unconscious self that must be redeemed and made conscious through the individuation process. Understood psychologically, Sophia would relate to the unconscious that is lost in the darkness and ignored by the ego, which, believing itself to be the only reality, corresponds to the false God who denies the true hidden God, the Self. If we equate Sophia with the collective unconscious then the lost Sophia is the unconscious whose redemption requires the conscious descent of the ego into the darkness of the inner world.

I believe this to be true, and that the symbolism presented by the Gnostic myths relates to the processes of individuation and the manifestation of the Self. But is there is a different interpretation that would apply to her as a psychoidal figure? Bear in mind that though there is the fallen Sophia, there always remains a higher Sophia, and one of her primary characteristics is that of the redeemer. As the lower Sophia she is the one in need of redemption, but as the higher Sophia she participates in the act of redemption. Thus, Sophia herself is split into two aspects of her being.

Gnosticism, and later alchemy, is about redemption, and it is the soul that must be redeemed. Sophia represents the feminine aspect of the psyche, the soul that has lost its roots and becomes split off from its source. The fallen Sophia in this sense is found within every human being for, according to the Gnostics, our souls are cut off from the true source. In a more psychoidal sense, Sophia is that aspect of God that has been split off from His higher aspects and lost in the material life. She is the gold lost and hidden in matter that the alchemists must extract and purify, not only for their own redemption but also for the redemption of the divine principal itself. The fall of Sophia marks the split within the divine world, and this split can be seen as the cause of all evil and of our entrapment, as human beings, in the sleeping state or unawareness of our divinity.

We have seen that the One Thing gives rise to psychoidal Names that personify aspects of Its nature and being. These forces in the psychoid should harmonize and cooperate, but they do not. Almost from the moment they enter the psychoid they seem to split apart and fall into disunion. It is this disunion that the lower Sophia represents. Her entrapment and rape illustrate the degree to which the forces of chaos have entered the psychoid. The archons and false gods are the psychoidal entities that will not acknowledge union or harmony as a goal, but insist on their own autonomy to the exclusion of all else. They seem to be actual psychoidal forces, but also represent the tendency in the Names to ignore each other and act simply as they will. Ibn Arabi commented that the Names seem not to be aware of each other's existence, a condition leading to chaos. Sophia is tainted by this condition of non-awareness, at least in part. The higher Sophia is the Wisdom of all things, including the other Names. It is perhaps for this reason that she unites first with God, creating the *filius* that acts as a center for the psychoidal world. In the processes of alchemy that prepare her for this union, Sophia undergoes purification, and the lower and upper parts of her come together. In creating the union between Sophia and God, the alchemist also heals Sophia. Students of the Kabbalah will recognize the similarities of this theme to that of the *Shekinah*: the lower, feminine aspect of God who is in exile with the people of Israel.

Jung summarizes this motif in his book *Psychology and Alchemy* when he writes, "alchemy is interested in the fate and manifest redemption of the substances, for in them the divine soul lies captive and awaits the redemption that is granted to it at the moment of release. The captive soul than appears in the form of the 'Son of God' [the Philosopher's Stone]. For the alchemists, the one primarily in need of redemption is not man, but the deity who is lost and sleeping in matter."[18] Sophia is the divine soul lost in matter.

Sophia's rape corresponds to the oppression of the feminine archetype in the patriarchal world. The loss of Sophia is the loss of all feminine values, and represents the domination of both material and spiritual life by the masculine principal that, in its one-sidedness, is truly the false god. But Sophia is also that which has been lost to God. God is incomplete and one-sided until Sophia is returned to him.

Sophia is the wisdom of all things and, like the Chinese Tao, reveals the path most in tune with an individual's nature. If individuals follow her bidding they discover who they are and how best to express themselves in the world. If a society consisted of individuals living with Sophia, that society would reach the highest cultural, moral, and spiritual levels. But, of course, very few individuals listen to Sophia. She is not honored nor is she respected: in fact, few would recognize her existence. As a psychoid being, she finds no home in our world. She is lost in unconsciousness and wanders the world looking for those who will know her. As I have seen repeatedly, a psychoidal being is transformed when a human being recognizes and relates to it. Without this recognition and relationship, it remains undeveloped and unfulfilled. Psychoidal alchemy is the means by which a psychoidal entity becomes whole unto itself. So long as people ignore Sophia she remains lost in the darkness and tainted by her lack of fulfillment.

On the other hand, as the Wisdom of God, Sophia is part of the whole divinity. Though autonomous, she belongs to the greater whole, and should be part of the greater whole. Since she is not, God has lost something of his own feminine nature and of his own wisdom. It is easy to see why evil would follow such a situation, for a one-sided God would function inadequately. If we take the Gnostic mythology seriously, there is something about creation itself that splits Sophia from her divine partner. Regardless of the origins of this split, there is no doubt that it exists. So long as it exists, not only do Sophia and God remained unfulfilled, the world itself remains lost in confusion. It is up to us to discover Sophia, restore her to herself, and then to God.

THE PERSONIFICATION OF SOPHIA

We have seen that Sophia is a divine hypostasis. Another word for *hypostasis* is "person," which implies that such a divine being personifies itself. As we saw in the first chapter, spiritual beings must personify themselves in order to manifest and relate to human beings. Personification, or taking on individual form, is a major part of otherworldly manifestation. We may turn to alchemy to find examples of Sophia's personification.

Alchemical allegories and dialogue form an essential part of alchemical literature. They are used to symbolically express the nature of substances and processes required for the creation of the Philosopher's Stone. They are often literary devices, but there are many examples of real visionary experiences and dialogue between the alchemists and spirits; enough, in fact, to convince us that such occurrences were part of the alchemical work. The depiction of Sophia as a person includes real experience as well as symbolic expression. The need to personify such a figure demonstrates her reality for the alchemist. Wisdom was not simply a metaphor for insight and learning, but was a real spirit whose blessing and revelations were necessary if an individual hoped to succeed in the laborious task of generating the Stone. Examining the way in which the alchemical writers personified Sophia proves helpful in understanding not only Sophia but the role that she played in alchemy as well.

Perhaps the most famous depiction of Sophia occurs in Michael Maier's *Atalanta Fugiens* as seen in figure 1 on page 28. The picture shows a

Figure 1. Sophia as depicted in Michael Maier's Atalanta Fugiens, *p. 157.*

beautiful woman with a crown on her head standing next to the Tree of Life. The epigram underneath the emblem reads:

> In Man's affairs, the greatest wisdom is
> The one from which calm wells and healthy life.
> Her right hand holds salubrious length of years,
> But in her left o'erwhelming treasures hide
> If one approaches her with head in hand,
> She'll be like fruit from off the tree of life.[19]

In the same work, Maier offers another depiction of Sophia illustrated here in figure 2 (page 29). In this emblem, Sophia is nature and is shown once more as a beautiful woman, this time guiding the alchemist on his quest. The alchemist, equipped with the lamp of intellectual study and the staff of reason, follows in her footsteps. Sophia as nature is the guide, and this emblem reminds the alchemist that the best course of action is to follow nature. In these two emblems Sophia personifies the guide and the source of the infinite treasures deriving from the tree of life itself. She is the mother of all creation and the bestower of the greatest gift of all, wisdom.

Figure 2. Sophia as guide. From Michael Maier's Atalanta Fugiens.

Figure 3 on page 30 is from 1785, and shows Sophia from whose breasts flow the red sulfur and the white mercury. The modern commentator on this illustration wrote, "Wisdom is the female emanation of God, through which his spiritual seed is realized, first in the uttered word of heavenly Sophia, then in matter through the world of nature. The latter is the fallen, lower Sophia, and is identified with mercury, the root of all metals."[20] This illustration and commentary indicate the equation of the lower Sophia with nature. They also indicate how the lower and higher Sophia cooperate in the work of creation.

Figure 4 on page 31, from 1516, is a miniature showing a winged and crowned nature who is looking angrily at the alchemist. We see the alchemical laboratory in the background, but nature, seated in the hollow of a strange-looking tree, seems angry indeed. Since nature personified is equated with Sophia, at least the lower Sophia, we may legitimately interpret the figure in the tree as Sophia. The bare breasts are a common image in the emblems of Sophia, for nakedness indicates the essential nature of a figure and the breasts are the source from which flow either the alchemical substances, mercury and sulfur, or inspiration and wisdom themselves. Notice also that the figure of nature is winged, indicating that she is a spiritual

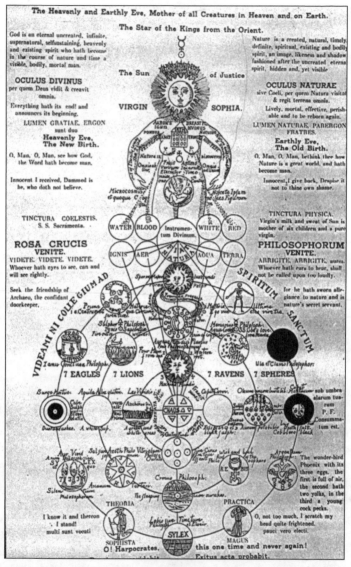

Figure 3. The Divine Sophia, from whose breasts flows the source of all life and whose flowing milk is the mercury of the philosophers. From Roob, Alchemy and Mysticism, *p. 502. Original is in* Geheime Figuren der Rosenkreuzer *(Altona, 1785).*

Figure 4. Sophia, seated in the tree of life, warns the alchemist who seeks the Philosopher's Stone that he will find it only with her help and never by studying books alone. Miniature painting by Jehan Perréal, painter at the court of Margaretha of Austria, 1516, reprinted from Roob, Alchemy and Mysticism, *p. 504.*

force, while her crown indicates her divinity. Her crown is composed of the symbols of all the planets and chemical substances, revealing that she contains the mystery of alchemy. She is angry with the alchemist for wasting time in his laboratory when it is she herself who holds the secrets of the great work. She says to the alchemist "You melt metals, burn atramentum, seal and break different vessels, build furnaces both large and small. In truth, I can assure you I am ashamed of your folly."[21]

In the *Aurora Consurgens* there are two pictures of Sophia, both of which relate to the themes in the preceding emblems. In figure 5 on page 33, we have an interesting image of Sophia, once more winged, standing on a black orb. One caption reads "turn to me with your whole heart and do not despise me because I am black and dark, for the sun has burned me so, and the black depths have covered my face."[22] This is a reference to the fallen or lower Sophia though the wings indicate she retains her spiritual nature. In her belly seems to be a kind of caduceus figure with two snakes wrapped around what appears to be a sword. The two snakes would once again refer to mercury and sulfur and the sword to the hidden fire or to the wisdom and discrimination Sophia possesses. In any case, this figure presents Sophia as containing the mystery of the work but as a being afraid of being rejected. In her womb, the creative center of the Goddess, lays the hidden treasure— the union of opposites that creates the Philosopher's Stone. Sophia, herself, will wed to create this Stone, but within herself she also unites the opposites and will give birth to the child of the philosophers.

In the last depiction of Sophia, figure 6 on page 33, we see her once more bare-breasted and crowned, suckling two alchemists. Her face is red and the caption relates this redness to the dawn beginning to lighten the darkness that dominates the background. The alchemists seemed to be deriving wisdom from the breasts of Sophia as well as sulfur and mercury. Sophia herself is the rising dawn whose bright countenance lights up the darkness of unconsciousness. To drink her milk is to partake of her wisdom and be lifted to the place of mysteries. As the previous emblem laid emphasis on her womb, this one stresses her breasts. In both cases, it is her feminine attributes that are empowered with the mystery and located as the source of wisdom.

In all of these emblems, Sophia is a beautiful woman, naked and containing within her own body the secrets of the work. She personifies not only wisdom but also all the ingredients needed in alchemy, for she is nature herself. She is clearly a living being and most decidedly a personification of the feminine divine. In some of the emblems, she is speaking to the

Figure 5. The winged (serpentine) Sophia, pregnant with the magical caduceus symbolized by the two snakes (the opposites) united around the sword of her power and authority. From the Aurora Consurgens, *reprinted from Roob,* Alchemy and Mysticism, *p. 239.*

Figure 6. Two alchemists nurse at Sophia's breasts, drinking her wisdom and love. From the Aurora Consurgens, *late 14th century, reprinted from Roob,* Alchemy and Mysticism, *p. 239.*

alchemist, which takes us to the next form of personification: a being with whom one can relate and dialogue.

Jacob Boehme had an intimate relationship with the divine being he believed to be Sophia. She apparently spoke to him quite often and he records some of these dialogues in his books. I believe them to be genuine dialogues and not teaching devices. Here is a short example of the type of dialogues he recorded:

> *The Soul Speaks Further to Its Nobel Sophia As to Itself in Its Own Regenerate Loveplay:*
>
> 48. Ah, my noble Pearl and Flame of my light opened in my anguished fire-life, how You changed me into Your joy. O beautiful Love, I broke my faith with You in my father Adam, and, by the fire's might I have changed myself into the pleasure and vanity of the external world. I took a foreign lover and I would have had to walk in a dark valley in a foreign love if You had not remained in great faith and come into the house of my misery through Your penetration and destruction of the wrath of God, hell and dark death, and had [not] brought Your meekness and love to my fire-life again.
>
> O sweet love, You have brought the waters of eternal life from out of God's fountain, and revived me in my great thirst. In You I see God's mercy that earlier my foreign love had hidden. In You I can be joyful. You've changed my fire-anguish into great joy. Ah gracious Love, give me Your pearl so that I may remain in such joy for ever.
>
> *Thereupon the Noble Sophia Replies to the Soul Again and Says:*
>
> 49. My dear lover and great treasure, your beginning gives me the greatest joy. Through the deep gates of God, through God's wrath, through hell and death I have broken into the house of your misery, and I have given you my love out of Grace, and released you from the chains and bonds by which you were bound fast.[23]

In this exchange the soul and Sophia pledge their love to one another and the soul asks Sophia for the great treasure of enlightenment symbolized here as the Pearl. Though Sophia later refuses because the soul may fall into darkness again and injure the Pearl, she promises to remain in the Heaven within. In this personification Sophia contains the secret of enlightenment and is the soul's lover and bride dwelling with it forever. Moreover, Sophia is the redeemer without whose help the soul would remain lost in the wrath of God.

As already noted, the alchemists personify Sophia as the giver of wisdom, without whose help they would never discover the secrets of their art. Often she chides them for not trusting her, but instead turning to their chemicals and mixtures. In the following dialogue, the alchemist discovers Wisdom by accident as he is recounting to himself all the woes and the suffering he has experienced in the alchemical pursuit:

> It seemed to me that the tree at the foot of which I was sitting suddenly cracked, which caused me to turn my head, and I perceived a nymph, an image of beauty, emerging from the tree. Her clothes were so light that they seemed transparent. She said to me: "I have understood from the bosom of this sacred tree the story of thy misfortunes. They are great doubtless, but such is the fate to which ambition led the youth who believed he could face every danger in order to satisfy his desires. I shall add no reflection so as not to aggravate thy misfortunes; I shall instead soothe them. My essence is celestial, you can even consider me as an efflux of the pole star. My power is such that I animate everything: I am the astral spirit, I give life to everything that breathes and grows,; I know everything. Speak: what can I do for you?"
>
> Oh, celestial nymph, I said to her, you can revive within me a heart struck down by misfortune by giving me only a faint notion concerning the organization of the universe, the immortality of the soul, and to obtain for me the means to attain to the knowledge of the Philosophers' Stone and the universal medicine. I have become a public laughingstock. My face has sagged beneath the enormous weight of misfortune. For mercy's sake, deign to give me the means to restore myself in my own eyes.
>
> "I am truly touched by thy painful existence," she answered me. "Listen, summon together all thy faculties and engrave in your memory the following recital which I shall give you. . . [24]

It is clear that Sophia once more is a figure possessing all the secrets of alchemy and in this case graciously invites the author to partake of her wisdom. But she is much more. She is the very essence of life and the astral spirit that gives life to all that breathes. She is the Great Mother, the *anima mundi*, and the soul-spark found in all things.

There are many more examples, but this should suffice to give you an idea of how alchemy viewed Sophia. She was the incarnation of the divine, a feminine being who was not only the wisdom of God but also a guide of souls, as well as all the operations and forces of nature. As nature and goddess of wisdom she was indispensable to any alchemist who hoped for success in the work. She reprimands those who seek in chemical devices to uncover her secrets, for those secrets are to be found in her alone. She possesses the pearl of great price that she bestows only on those she has chosen. As nature herself, she embodies not only all natural developments but all the alchemical components and processes, as well. In addition to this, she is a beautiful, numinous, feminine spirit who brings with her love to those who receive her.

THE LOVE OF SOPHIA

Closely related to the theme of Sophia as a personification is that of the love relationship that can develop between her and the alchemist. The third motif, therefore, is that of love.

Love is a very important theme in alchemy, one that has not been studied enough. It binds the opposites together and it helps to motivate the alchemists on their quest. Certainly, the idea of Sophia as a divine lover began before alchemy and can be found in the *Wisdom of Solomon* in which it is written, "a spirit of wisdom came to me. I preferred her above sceptre and throne, and held riches as nought by comparison; I reckoned no priceless gem her equal, since all gold in her sight is but a pinch of sand, and before her silver is accounted as clay. I loved her above health and shapeliness, and preferred her to the light of day."[25]

In the alchemical *Treatise of Salt*, the author wrote that the creation of the Stone was a proof of God's grace rather than an end in itself. The creator of the stone may rest assured that he not only possesses the greatest treasure in the world, but has received a token of God's love, and the "promise which divine Wisdom (who gives such a gift) has made in his favor, to accord him forever an eternal dwelling with her, and a perfect union in a celestial marriage, which we desire with all our heart for all Christians; for it is the center of all treasures."[26]

The author sees Sophia as his future spouse, his celestial partner with whom he will dwell forever. Recall that the gender of the alchemist would make no difference in this experience of Sophia. Man or woman would behold in her an eternal love and an eternal companion. For Boehme as well, Sophia was a companion in this life and a spouse in the next. The mystic wedding takes place between the human being and Sophia, and, according to Boehme, any who seeks her love will find it:

> Beloved Soul, if thou wilt be earnest without Intermission, thou shalt certainly obtain the Favor of a *Kiss* from the *Noble Sophia* (*or Divine Wisdom*) in the Holy Name JESUS; for She standeth ever before the Door of the *Soul, knocking,* and warning the Sinner of his wicked Way. Now if it once thus desireth Her Love, She is ready for it and *kisseth* it with the Beams of Her Sweet Love, from whence the Heart receiveth Joy.[27]

In all her might, in all her glory, Sophia nevertheless embraces the human soul with love. She not only loves the human being but she is loved in return. She is the greatest treasure in life and offers the promise of eternal union. The love of wisdom, so clearly present in the above quotes, finds its most ecstatic expression in the *Aurora Consurgens,* as we shall have occasion to see.

Sophia and the Ally

Sophia is the essence of wisdom and love for all souls. She raises a person to flights of ecstatic wonder and bliss and yet she includes the ordinary and the mundane. No other spirit, aside from the ally, inspires so much love, and for many it is this love that encourages them to undertake the rigors of inner alchemy and go through the hardships that such a path entails. For one caught in the love of Sophia the goal becomes union with her. The Philosopher's Stone, to be complete, must include union with her. This union exists not only between the human soul and Sophia, but also between Sophia and the masculine aspect of the divinity. Love exists between the masculine god and Sophia as much as between Sophia and her human partner. After all, alchemy finds its completion in the *coniunctio* between Sophia and her masculine counterpart, for the Stone is the embodiment of wisdom and power. The product of this union is the ally, or the *filius*. The ally, without Sophia, would lack the fullest capacity to relate and to love and would be incapable of completing its union with its chosen individual. The ally always contains within itself Sophia, for Sophia is its mother, as the masculine aspect of power is its father. Lyndy Abraham, in speaking of wisdom, writes that the " Philosopher's Stone or pure love essence is born of the union of power and wisdom. . . . Wisdom is the female aspect of the Philosopher's Stone or universal medicine."[28]

Alchemy, unlike many other traditions, works within the material world and seeks the divinity in that world. The alchemist seeks to uncover the spirit hidden within matter, liberate it and unite that liberated spirit with the spirit of the higher world. For some, like the Gnostic, the materialization of spirit was a grave error, but for the alchemist this materialization produces the wonders and mysteries of nature. In either case, the materialization of spirit is closely related to Sophia.

According to Henry Khunrath, at the moment of the creation, the spirit of God moved upon the waters and filled the world, entering the virgin womb and center of the earth, "the most misticall broodie Mother of the greate world, bodily it is become a Corporall Salt of wisdome. . ."[29] The salt of wisdom is the body into which spirit incarnates and there is a correlation between Sophia and salt, which Jung noticed and wrote about. He quotes Irenaeus who, in reporting the views of the Gnostic, wrote that "the spiritual, they say, (is) sent forth to this end, that, being united here below with the psychic, it may take form, and be instructed simultaneously by intercourse with it. And this they declare to be the salt and the light of the world."[30] He also quotes Hippolytus as follows:

> this wave is raised from the water by the wind and made pregnant
> in its nature, and has received within itself the reproductive power
> of the feminine, it retains the light scattered from on high together
> with the fragrance of the spirit . . . and that is Nous given shape in
> various forms. This (light) is a perfect God, who is brought down
> from the unbegotten light on high and from the spirit into man's
> nature as into a temple, by the power of nature . . . it is . . . as if it
> were of the salt of all created things.[31]

In this quote the process of incarnation is correlated with the mystery of nature and the salt of all created things. Jung comments on this passage that it is strangely beautiful and contains "pretty well everything that the alchemists endeavored to say about salt: it is the spirit, the turning of the body into light (*albedo*), the spark of the anima mundi, imprisoned in the dark depths of the sea."[32] The reproductive power of nature belongs to Sophia, and she is thus instrumental in the incarnation of spirit and the spiritualization of the body. Jung later quotes Johannes Grasses as saying that the lead of the Philosopher's Stone contains "the shining white dove, named the salt of the metals, wherein is the whole magistery of the work. This [dove] is the pure, chaste, wise, and rich queen of Sheba."[33] I interpret the queen of Sheba as being Sophia.

Salt is generally the principle by which incarnation occurs, and contains within it the highest concentration of divine light. From what has been said, it is clear that salt and wisdom are closely related, and that one of Sophia's functions is to both incarnate the spirit and spiritualize the body.

Jacob Boehme is even more explicit about the connection between Sophia and the incarnation of the body. Unfortunately, his writing is very complex and difficult to understand and he has a tendency to make up his own terms to describe certain spiritual and psychoidal events. Essentially, he states that God is invisible though perceptible in some way, while Sophia is visible. She has a body that Boehme calls *Ternarius Sanctus* or the holy earth; and into this holy "Ternary" God enters. Through this union of God and Sophia as a substantial body there "is become one Thing, not in spirit, but in substance, as body, and soul."[34] This is a remarkable passage in that it equates Sophia with the principle that gives body to God. From the perspective of psychoidal alchemy, Sophia is the means by which spirit takes on substance and form.

I have argued in the previous chapter that psychoidal alchemy naturally works with psychoidal spirits, and it now seems that Sophia is responsible for the union of incorporeal spirit with some form of body, which, though different from the physical body, has substance and form. The assumption of subtle matter by the spirit marks its entry into the world of the Gnostic imagination, or the psychoid world. Sophia is closely connected with imagination; in fact, Boehme wrote that she is "a divine imagination."[35]

Boehme also suggests that the ternary further incarnates in the Virgin Mary.[36] If we take Boehme's idea and remove it from his Christian theology, and expand it to include psychoidal processes in general, we can argue that a twofold incarnation takes place. There is first an incarnation from the divine realm into the so-called ternary, which is the body of Sophia, and from there into the human psyche. Sophia is the middle ground and the body of the psychoid. This remarkable concept that Sophia is the body through which spirit incarnates into the psychoid and then, as psychoidal, moves into the psyche, explains her connection to salt which is the alchemical principle of incarnation. It also demonstrates that Sophia is indispensable for the correct performance of alchemical processes, for without her, just as without salt, there is no way for spirit to become matter. Moreover, it demonstrates that she is the middle world between spirit and world, a middle position occupied by the world of imagination.

Sophia is thus related to the incarnation of spirit in the psychoid world, but what of the spiritualization of matter, which was an important goal of the alchemist? To understand this process we must turn to Paracelsus. His philosophy of Sophia is not always clear, but he seems to be saying that there are two feminine principles within nature that correspond to the higher and lower Sophia. The feminine divine principal "in nature is the elements in a passive state and Sophia in an active one."[37] The "labor sophiae" or Sophia's work activates and transforms the elements in such a way that they yield a second paradise in which there is no disease. The material elements are affected by transcendent means to create a new paradise and the elements are, in turn, spiritualized. Through the work of Sophia matter is therefore spiritualized. The writings of Paracelsus on Sophia need further study, as does the correlation between them and the idea of Sophia held by other alchemists. However, it appears that Sophia is related to the materialization of spirit and the spiritualization of matter. As a psychoidal being, she is the principle, or gateway, through which psychoidal alchemy is achieved. Other spirits wishing to enter the psychoidal realm must pass through Sophia. As shall become apparent when we study the *Aurora*, Sophia is often related to the body of immortality, or the subtle body. Through her spiritualization of matter, it transforms and becomes psychoidal. She thus seems to be the pivotal force in psychoidal alchemy. It therefore is natural that the alchemists believed that she was related to all the processes of alchemy.

Broadly speaking, Sophia's relationship with alchemical processes consists of two main parts: Sophia knows the secrets of the alchemical operations as well as the actual means by which those operations are performed. These two attributes are often discussed together in the same text. For example, Simon Forman wrote that "All the sciences of the world, O Son are comprehended in this my hidden Wisdom; and this, and the learning of the Art, consists in these wonderful hidden elements which it doth discover and complete."[38] Moreover, if the alchemists follow their understanding with correct procedures, Wisdom brings those procedures to fruition, or as Forman comments "Wisdom proceeds onwards to the fulfillment of her Law."[39] That is to say, if the right method is combined with the right ingredients in accordance with the teachings of Wisdom, the end result must be successful, for so Wisdom decrees. Artephius, a well-known early alchemist, wrote:

> For this cause sake, they have passed over into one another, and by the influence of wisdom, are converted into one another. O Wisdom: how thou makest the most fixed gold to be volatile and fugitive, yea, though by nature it is the most fixed of all things in the world.[40]

Wisdom, in addition to revealing the secrets of the art, governs and empowers the operations by which one performs the art. It is Wisdom, therefore, that is responsible for the performance of the work through which the Stone is created. Rather than attempting to control the alchemical processes, the good alchemists allow them to unfold naturally and according to the dictates of Wisdom. Following nature also means dialoguing with and learning from Sophia, who is the psychoidal personification of nature as well as the higher Wisdom that guides nature. It is no wonder, therefore, that so many alchemists do active imagination work with Sophia.

.   .   .

Sophia is a divine being who guides all creation in its course and even advises God in what needs to be done. She knows the essence of all beings and the proper path that they must follow. She is the guide who helps us redeem nature and the divinity itself, as well as our individual souls. She is therefore both the Redeemer and that which must be redeemed. She is a living, psychoidal being with whom we can form a relationship of the deepest love that can lead to union and, through this union, elevation to a higher state of being. She is the means by which spirit becomes matter and matter becomes spirit, and even God incarnates in her body. It is this being that the *Aurora Consurgens* so vividly describes. And it is to this description that we now turn.

CHAPTER 3

AURORA CONSURGENS AND PSYCHOIDAL ALCHEMY

The author of the *Aurora Consurgens* seems to have written it in a rush of enthusiasm, for his words come forth with great emotion. The text includes a series of quotes from the Bible concerning Sophia and then one or two alchemical references. The author assimilates these biblical quotations in his fevered effort to describe what he has experienced, and then to place that experience within the alchemical context. This procedure makes for a strange juxtaposition of alchemical operations and biblical imagery. For example, the author begins his work with the following:

> All good things come to me together with her, that Wisdom of the south, who preacheth abroad, who uttereth her voice in the streets, crieth out at the head of the multitudes, and in the entrance of the gates of the city uttereth her words, saying: Come to me and be enlightened, and your operations shall not be confounded; all ye that desire me shall be filled with my riches. Come (therefore) children, hearken to me; I will teach you the science of God.[1]

Keeping in mind all that we have learned about Sophia, statements such as this make sense. It is not surprising that all good things come with her, for she is the Wisdom of God, the feminine principal who brings to the alchemists all the riches that Wisdom can offer. That all good things come with her means, in effect, that she is all good things, and that Wisdom above all else is that which is to be desired. We must not assume the writer understood Wisdom as abstract knowledge as such. For him, Wisdom was a feminine incarnation with whom he related and whom he quite clearly loved. "Wisdom of the south" (*sapienta austri*) is a designation apparently referring to the Queen of Sheba who, as von Franz points out, appears occasionally in the literature of alchemy as an author of alchemical texts. *Austri* in Latin actually means not just the south but the south wind, so we can understand the south wind as a reference to Sophia.[2]

Von Franz amplifies the south wind quite extensively in her book, pointing out that Christ is called king of the south and God Himself "shall go with the whirlwind of the South."[3] According to her, the south wind is also a symbol of the Holy Spirit, and as the south wind is hot and dry, this reference has to do with the fire of love related to the Holy Spirit. Arabian alchemy calls the sublimation process the great south wind, which refers to the heating of the retort (alchemical crucible) and its contents. Von Franz concludes by saying that wisdom of the south is a "feminine pneuma who enkindles and inspires the author at his work. She is a spirit of truth bringing him enlightenment. Thus the anima appears here not as a personal content but in her transpersonal collective significance as the feminine complement of the god image itself."[4]

There are other amplifications in alchemy relating to the south wind. In the *Turba Philosophorum* it is written that, "know ye that a very great wind of the south, when it is stirred up, sublimates clouds and elevates the vapours of the sea."[5] Philalethes, the author of *The Fount of Chemical Truth* wrote:

> In the South-west there is a high mountain (very near the Sun), one of seven, and the second in height. This mountain is of a very hot temperature (because it is not far from the Sun), and in this mountain is enclosed a vapor or spirit, whose services are indispensable for our work. But it does not ascend, unless it is quickened, nor is it quickened unless you dig knee-deep on the summit of the mountain. If you do this, a subtle exultation (or spirit) ascends, and is congealed by the air into drops of beautifully limpid water—which is our water, our fire, our vessel, and our furnace.[6]

Another alchemists wrote that the ignorant "do not recognize the seed in germ of all metals, with a glowing Mercury of nature lies hidden, the seed which the south wind provides in shining gray, viscous liquid form."[7]

Sophia is a spirit of truth inspiring the author in his work and bringing with her great riches of a spiritual nature. She, like the Holy Spirit, like Christ, and like God, is in the south. But in addition, the material that I have adduced indicates quite clearly that Sophia is the hidden spirit in matter equated with the *anima mundi*, with Mercury, and with fire. This hidden spirit, closely related to the lower Sophia, is the *prima materia*, or the secret substance that the alchemist must discover to perform their work. She is both spirit and matter, but must be discovered and released. When she is released, transformations follow.

That which is dug from the mountain is therefore the *prima materia* conceived here as a certain vapor or spirit which quickens and governs all life. It is in essence the principle of all existence. It is because of this great power to animate all things that the alchemists sought to isolate and concentrate it, so that it would bring to life the hidden power within metals and within the human being itself. As Wisdom, Sophia is thus the very heart of life and is in this way closely related to the *anima mundi*. Wisdom therefore is a secret of matter, and the secret of life itself. Figure 7 shows the dwarf miners at work digging the *prima materia* from the mountain. From the ore the miners extracted, they would make their mercury and sulfur and set in motion the procedures leading to the creation of the Philosopher's Stone. The pelican in the background refers to the deeper processes of alchemy in their earlier stages.

There are probably many ways that the alchemists sought to discover Wisdom in her role as the soul of creation, and to extract that soul for their own work. But the author of the *Aurora* imagines that she is a living being whom one can love and who bestows the secrets of the alchemical work on her beloved. This means that the soul of the world personifies itself, which

Figure 7. Digging for the prima materia.

in turn makes it possible to work with her through imaginal encounters. If we imagine talking to Sophia as the south wind, she could tell us about that which brings life to matter, or about what enlivens our own being, and could show us how to concentrate the spirit of life to create transformations of all kinds. So von Franz is correct in saying that Sophia brings enlightenment, but the reason that she brings enlightenment is that she not only holds the secret of the *prima materia*, she herself is the *prima materia*, the very essence of the Stone, and this essence is the spirit of life itself.

We can only grasp Sophia in an approximate way. The symbols that we are encountering, however, reveal that she is the *prima materia* and explain in part why the author of the *Aurora* focuses all his attention on her, for she is in herself the secret of the Stone. Without her, the Stone would lack life and the capacity to create transformation, and would not possess the wisdom that it imparts to the alchemist.

ANIMA MUNDI

In a very real sense, the worldview of the alchemists was of a psychoidal nature. The physical universe was the body, while the *anima mundi* was its soul. All physical objects and every human being shared parts of the world soul. The alchemists repeat endlessly that the *anima mundi* exists within the human psyche. For example, Sigismund Bacstrom wrote that, "The soul of Man as well as all rational Spirits (the Angels) consist (according to their primitive Essence) of the Spirit of the World or Anima Mundi and the power of reasoning."[8] Bacstrom also asserts that this universal spirit is the force that makes nature operate and is the *prima materia* out of which the Stone is created:

> In the Beginning God created the Universal Spirit or the Universal Agent of Nature, the Soul of the Universe.
>
> This is the first emanation of Divine Light; it is a unity and immortal, capable of manifesting itself, when moved or agitated, into Light and Fire. It is multipliable and yet is and remains but one. It is Omnipresent and yet occupies no visible space or room, except when manifested or multiplied in its third principle, Fire.
>
> It has the power of becoming material and of returning again to universality.[9]

In this quotation, which is representative of the views of a great many alchemists, the importance of the *anima mundi* is made clear. Like Sophia herself, the first element of creation is the universal spirit, or soul of the world. It is an emanation of light, immortal and capable of manifesting itself in light and fire. Though it remains a unity it is capable of multiplying itself and is a feminine being. Jung clearly expresses the identification of the *anima mundi* with Sophia when he writes that, "For the alchemists it [the original matter] was wisdom and knowledge, truth and spirit, and its source was in the inner man, though its symbol was common water or sea-water, What [sic] they evidently had in mind was a ubiquitous and All-pervading arcanum, an *anima mundi* and the 'greatest treasure,' the inner most and most secret numinosum of man."[10]

Bacstrom's description is remarkable in one other way. He states that the universal spirit has the power to either become material or to return to the spiritual, and that when it manifests materially it does so through fire and light. This capacity to move between the spirit and the material marks the *anima mundi* as psychoidal, since it must be viewed as something other than either matter or spirit. Sophia gives life to all things and can move between the worlds of matter and spirit. This reminds us of Boehme's statement that it is Sophia who gives substance to all the spirits, including God. Sophia, as *anima mundi*, relates to the world of the imagination and its power to incarnate spirits within the psyche as well as within the psychoid. The author of *The Waterstone of the Wise* puts it this way:

> [T]hey ascribe to it infinite Divine power and virtue when they say that it is the Spirit of the Lord who fills the Universe, and in the beginning moved upon the face of the waters. They also call it the spirit of truth that is hid in the world, and cannot be understood without the inspiration of the Holy Spirit, or the teaching of those who know it. It is found potentially everywhere, and in everything, but in all its perfection and arcanum only in one thing. In short, it is a Spiritual Essence which is neither celestial nor infernal, but an aerial, pure, and precious body, in the middle between the highest and lowest, the choicest and noblest thing under heaven. But by the ignorant and the beginner it is thought to be the vilest and meanest of things.[11]

The description in this quotation of the *anima mundi* is all but identical with the description of the Philosopher's Stone, and it is clear that the *anima mundi* is the secret *prima materia*. Notice, too, that the author locates her in the middle place, being a spiritual essence neither celestial nor infernal, in other words, belonging neither to heaven nor to the underworld. This quotation reaffirms the psychoidal nature of the spirit of the world.

The spirit of the world, or *anima mundi* is a great mystery, and forms part of the psychoidal worldview in two ways. It is in and of itself a psychoidal being, and as the animating principle of the world is neither spirit nor matter. Furthermore, it is the special power sought by the alchemists from which they hoped to create the Philosopher's Stone. In this sense, the Stone would be the *anima mundi* transformed, purified, and multiplied in power and effectiveness. Psychoidal alchemy seeks to discover and work with Sophia as the *anima mundi*.

THE PROMISE OF SOPHIA

The *Aurora Consurgens* is in some ways unique in its presentation of the *prima materia* and the *anima mundi* in a personified form. Yet most alchemists imagined the *anima mundi* as a living being of some kind, and it is important to recognize that the work with the hidden divine force in matter could take the form of a relationship with the divinity. It is often easy to lose sight of the fact that the alchemists were not manipulating substances but relating to spirits and seeking to achieve their goals through these relationships. It is for this reason that much of the *Aurora* takes the form of a dialogue between Sophia and the alchemist.

At the beginning of the *Aurora*, the author relates Sophia's promise to bestow enlightenment and, if the alchemists come to her, that their operations will not be "confounded," that they will be filled with riches, and she will teach them the "science of God." It is not always an easy thing in this text to tell who is speaking, for the author moves quickly between the voices of Sophia, his own voice, and the voice of a masculine aspect of God that has not yet appeared. Immediately after the promise given by Sophia, he reverts back to his own voice, and explains that men and children pass her by daily in the streets and trot her into the mire. As this dialogue shows, we must be careful to discern which voice is speaking. In this case, Sophia makes a promise and the alchemist moves to a comment on that vow. What exactly does she pledge?

Sophia's promise reveals her two essential characteristics within the alchemical context. In the first place, she is able to offer enlightenment because, as Wisdom, she knows all things, especially the workings of the spirit within nature. After all, she was the agency through which creation took place, and she understands fully the natural course of things.

"Enlightenment" is a very strong word that indicates the transmission of knowledge that will allow the alchemists to gain insight into the secret of matter and its relationship to spirit. Enlightenment also refers to discovering the divine secrets that Sophia can impart.

Her second promise is that the operations of the alchemists will not be confounded. Anyone who studies alchemy for even a short time will know what a great promise this is, for accounts of alchemical processes often report failure. But a relationship with Sophia allows them to work properly since, as the spirit of nature, she allows the processes to unfold according to the natural course.

What does that mean for us when we engage in psychoidal alchemy today? It defines the key to success as the ability to form a relationship with the psychoidal being, Sophia. Her invitation in this text seems to be to everyone, but the ability to experience her is clearly not an easy one to cultivate. The hard part is developing the inner vision that would allow us to see the spirit that lies within the material world and to experience the spirit according to its psychoidal nature. In order to form a relationship with Sophia, we must be able to see and hear her, and this takes years of practice. Though spontaneous visions certainly occur, the capacity to relate to the psychoid on a regular basis is one that must be earned. As I indicated in chapter one, the practice of meditation and active imagination is essential in developing visionary aptitude. Through this skill we can perceive and learn to experience a relationship with Sophia. Forming a relationship with her allows us to experience the divine force not only within our own psyches but also in the world around us. She provides insight into the way in which matter reflects spirit and spirit governs matter, and the ways in which the divinity itself transforms.

Her final promise in the opening paragraph of the *Aurora* is that she will teach the science of God. The science of God is alchemy, but alchemy conceived of not as the pursuit of gold but as the study of all things divine. The wisdom that she offers is the knowledge of the psychoid and the ways in which matter and spirit interact and affect each other. Moreover, hers is the knowledge through which the spirit hidden in matter may be first discovered and then concentrated in the Philosopher's Stone.

The *Aurora*'s author wonders, after hearing Sophia's promise, who is wise enough to understand this, for men and children "pass her by daily in the streets in public places, and she is trodden into the mire by beasts of burden."[12] Our author, whom for the sake of convenience I shall call Thomas, quotes the alchemist known as Senior that, "Nought is more base in appearance then she, and nought is more precious in nature than she. . . ."[13] The theme of the *prima materia*, the most precious substance in the world, being despised and ignored is common in alchemy, as is the phrase that the Stone is found in the dung heap.

The precious substance is of mean appearance and looks worthless and useless. Thus, in *The Glory of the World*, it is written that "it is esteemed the vilest and meanest of earthly things. It is cast away and rejected by all."[14] Another alchemist writes:

> Having been deemed a worthless thing,
>   Although all the power lieth in it.
> Some know not how to separate it
>   From their Cortibus, therefore they fail.
> It was cast behind the door,
>   But the Wise Man taketh it up again. . .[15]

To the eyes of the untrained the spiritual essence that forms the basis of the work appears worthless and of no value. What does this motif mean? On one hand, thinking as an alchemist, the *prima materia* may be found in anything, but is so buried within matter that it is invisible to ordinary eyes. Moreover, in its natural state it is worthless because it must first be abstracted from the matter in which it rests. It must then be purified, made into spirit, and then returned to a purified material form before it is of any value in the alchemical undertaking. When Thomas says that Sophia is of no value, his statement reconnects her to the image of the *prima materia* and reminds us once again that she is the essence of the Stone. His language would be familiar to any alchemists, and they would immediately recognize Sophia as the *prima materia*.

Yet, this does not seem to interpret this motif completely. In what sense would the wisdom of God be worthless? Why would this most prized and magnificent being appear "base" as Senior says? Once more this reinforces the identification of Sophia with the Stone. The Stone is the most despicable of all things and the most precious, and therefore unites within itself all opposites. The same might be said of Sophia. There is always not only the upper, beautiful, and numinous Sophia, but the lower Sophia as well. The latter is base and ugly, and lost in the darkness of matter.

If one relates to Sophia as a psychoidal being, she incarnates the world's soul; a specific spirit that may be perceived at certain times by certain people. The revelation of this spirit does not belong to visionaries alone. I have known many people who have had visions of the spirit of the world. Bear in mind that when we are dealing with psychoidal alchemy, we are not simply talking symbolically. It does us no good to say that the baseness of Sophia symbolizes the ignorance of the world, or the fact that spirit is lost in the trivial existence that most people live. This may be true symbolically, but it does not tell us what the essence of baseness would be for a being such as Sophia. Only experience of the psychoidal entity could reveal her "baseness." The inner alchemist who wishes to perceive the psychoidal realm most especially wishes to perceive the spirit of the world, for it is that with which alchemy is performed. Sophia is the spirit of the world, but another way of understanding the spirit of the world is that it is the *prima materia*. As the *prima materia*, she has no form, no shape; no particular way of expressing herself—she is pure chaos. Martin Ruland wrote, "the Hermetic Chemists have compared their work to the development of the universe out of the primeval chaos"[16] When we first encounter the spirit of the world, it is completely chaotic, and in its chaos it is threatening and overwhelming as well as "base." This is the wild dragon who must be slain at the beginning of the alchemical work, for its chaos is deadly poison to the human being.

All psychoidal figures emerge from this chaos, but sometimes, as explorers of the psychoid, we encounter only the chaos. This can be harmful both to psyche and body, and it is only with the greatest effort that we can perceive, within the chaos, the beauty of the beings that may materialize from within it. Sophia is the universal spirit, the *anima mundi* who contains all things. Nevertheless, her first appearance can, in fact, be most trying and painful. If she appears as the lower Sophia, the alchemist experiences her agony, confusion, and a deadening sense of chaos. Psychoidal alchemy requires that the alchemist learn to hold the tension between this chaos and the feelings that the psychoidal figure can convey, and not be overwhelmed by it. When Sophia appears as the numinious upper Sophia all is well, but she cannot deny her lower nature and the alchemist must be willing to experience this as profoundly as he does her upper nature. If he is willing to see her as she is, then he heals her and begins her process of redemption. The opposites within her nature must be united so that she becomes a whole being. It is only through the efforts of the alchemist that she finds healing and wholeness. The inner alchemist brings to the work the capacity to withstand the pain and tension of looking into the face of chaos, and trusting that from within it will emerge the most precious of all things.

Thomas cannot remain with Sophia's baseness for very long, nor can anyone who once glimpses her inner nature. We are compelled to seek experiences of the transcendent Wisdom that she incarnates. But it is important not to skip over the baseness too quickly. I have seen many people experience the chaos of the psychoid in dramatic ways and, because they expected ecstasy and a vision into the order of the universe, they were convinced that they had gone wrong in their explorations. In fact, they had found what they were seeking, and should have fixed their gaze on this chaos, withstood the agony it produced, and waited for the order to emerge. If we believe we have gone wrong, we will flee from the chaos before the harmony appears. This is not to say that all first experiences of psychoidal energy are chaotic. Sometimes it will appear formed and harmonious in its initial experience, but it cannot remain that way until the alchemical processes have unfolded. The pain that the experiences of such chaos causes us is a reminder of the fallen state of Sophia, in which her spirit is locked away in cosmic chaos.

But Thomas moves quickly back to a description of the powerful Sophia, and the ecstasy Thomas feels when he describes her is neither inappropriate nor inflated:

> She it is that Solomon chose to have instead of light, and above all beauty and health; in comparison of her he compared not unto her the virtue of any precious stone. For all gold in her sight shall be esteemed as a little sand, and silver shall be counted as clay; and this is not without cause, for to gain her is better than the merchandise of silver and the most pure gold. And her fruit is more precious than all the riches of this world, and all things that are desired are not to be compared with her. Length of days and health are in her right hand, and in her left hand glory and infinite riches. Her ways are beautiful operations and praiseworthy, not unsightly nor ill-favored . . . she is a tree of life to them that lay hold on her, and an unfailing light.[17]

There is much to learn about Sophia in this ecstatic passage, including a few paradoxes. To begin with, Thomas states that Solomon chose her instead of the light, and yet the concluding sentence states that she is an unfailing light, which means that to choose her is to choose the light. In order to understand this paradox we must examine the symbolism of light in alchemy.

Light is one of the most common images within most spiritual traditions and almost always denotes a spiritual essence of some kind. There is, for example, the role that light plays within Sufism, as Henry Corbin points out in his book on the man of light.[18] It is also a pregnant image in alchemical literature. Correlation of light with wisdom is often plainly expressed.

One alchemist speaks of a divine being, second only to God, whose power permeates all of creation. We cannpot understand this power, but imagine it to be a star:

> It is called the Star of Wisdom and an eternal Light, this is the reason, because it is Light in itself, and borrows nothing from others, but rather communicates to them a virtue, and because the foundation of wisdom is hid therein, words are wanting to me to express the virtue and the power that do lie hid in it.[19]

According to this author, wisdom is a light that contains within itself all virtues and powers, and communicates them to others, needing nothing in return. It contains all the creative power of the spirit in a mystery that cannot be explained.

Light is also related to the Philosopher's Stone, and Jung goes so far as to say that the idea of the light "coincides with the concept of Sapientia and Scientia. We can safely call light the central mystery of philosophical alchemy."[20]

This central mystery of light has many different dimensions to it. In the first place, it relates to Wisdom herself, who seems to be a light. In addition, there is what is called the light of nature, which is closely correlated to wisdom, for it bestows insight upon the alchemists. For example, in the *Waterstone of the Wise*, the author writes that "by the light of Nature, and Divine revelation, they intuitively perceived that the Almighty, in His love to men, must have concealed in the world some wonderful arcanum by which every imperfect, diseased, and defective thing in the whole world might be renewed, and restored to its former vigour."[21] The light of nature refers to an inner source of spiritual understanding that, in an intuitive way, enlightens the alchemists and gives them insight into the mysterious substances with which they work. As the quote indicates, the light of nature is closely related to divine revelation, and sometimes the two seem inseparable.

Light is also often associated with the divinity. "From the beginning of all things God is. He is likened to light and fire. . . ."[22] George Ripley calls God "O most Incomprehensible Light."[23] The light of nature and the light of the divine often play the same role by revealing the truth which the alchemist must have, for "unless the Mind be kindled with a Beam of Divine Light, it will not be able to penetrate this most hidden Science . . ."[24]

Light is therefore clearly related to Sophia as wisdom and the giver of wisdom. Sophia's relationship to light also links her to God. Johannes Helmond sums up this correlation best when he says that the kingdom of

the divine spirit is formed out of the purest light "and the eternal primor-
dial pictures which . . . reveal only infallible truth and wisdom."[25] At the
same time, light is part of psychoidal alchemy, for light represents the spirit
that can have a tremendous impact upon matter. As one writer puts it, "he
that can by light draw light out of things, or multiply light with light, he
knows how to add the universal spirit of life to the particular spirit of life,
and by this addition do miracles."[26] In other words, light is not only revealed
knowledge but also acts upon matter itself. Experiences of light often
accompany healing events.

In traditions such as the Kabbalah, light is seen as the essence of the
divinity that flows from one world to the next. Moreover, light is the form
in which psychoidal entities can appear, and beings of light are divine or
angelic creatures in almost every spiritual tradition in the world.

Why, then, does Thomas first reject the light in order to accept Sophia
when later he states that Sophia and light are the same? It seems to me that
what Thomas is saying is that he so loves Sophia that he rejects anything and
everything unless it comes with her. He rejects the light if it does not come
as Sophia; he rejects gold and silver if they do not come with Sophia, and,
as he finally states, "her fruit is more precious than all the riches of this
world, and all things that are desired are not to be compared with her." He
knows that she can bring gold and silver and great riches, but it is not for
this reason that he loves her. His ecstasy grows not for what Sophia can
bring, but for who Sophia is. His ecstasy is like that of the lover who has
fallen in love with a rich and powerful entity whom he knows is capable of
the greatest miracles. But in his sight, all of these things, even the divine
light, are nothing as compared to Sophia herself.

The alchemical processes in Thomas's writings are neither about the
creation of gold, nor even about the Philosopher's Stone *per se*—they are
about Sophia and his love for her. He wishes to know her, to transform
her, and to enter into union with her. His ecstasy is the ecstasy of the lover,
and all of his operations are aimed at creating union with his beloved. In
the alchemy of Thomas, as in the alchemy of many others, the goal is the
incarnation of and the creation of union with the beloved. Though not all
alchemists named the beloved Sophia, their relationship with the
Philosopher's Stone by whatever name is often rooted in love. Psychoidal
alchemy is not simply about liberating spirit trapped in matter, but about
empowering, incarnating, and relating to a psychoidal entity.

In her commentary, Dr. von Franz is concerned that Thomas is
inflated when he gives voice to his ecstasy, or that perhaps the unconscious

has overwhelmed him. What von Franz in her interpretation seems to forget is how often love engenders ecstasy. Thomas's ecstatic outpourings resemble mystical poetry, and have little to do with invasions of the unconscious. No one can perceive the psychoid nor relate to a psychoidal entity without ecstasy of one degree or another. It is within this context that we must understand the seemingly endless outpourings that Thomas voices. If we can keep this context in mind and remember that alchemy is about the beloved, we will find ourselves able to penetrate the mysteries of the *Aurora* with greater ease.

Tree Symbolism

Thomas goes on to state that Wisdom is the Tree of Life to those who lay hold of her. Jung found the symbolism of the tree important enough to write a whole essay on it. Looking at some of the motifs related to the tree will shed some more light on Sophia. Jung summarizes his study of the tree by stating that it relates to the self, to wholeness, and the processes of life and of alchemy. He argues that the alchemist was less interested in the world tree and more interested in the tree as the individuation process. He also makes it very clear that tree is correlated to wisdom.[27]

The alchemists often used the image of the tree and its growth to signify the transformation of the material in the retort. Many claimed to see a tree grow in the vessel, which they took as a sign of transformation and progression toward the creation of the Philosopher's Stone. An early example of the use of the tree is found in the *Turba Philosophorum*:

> A certain person, who has followed science, has notified to me after what manner he discovered this same tree, and appropriately operating, did extract the fruit and eat of it. . . . he said: Take that tree, and build a house about it, which shall wholly surround the same, which shall also be circular, dark, encircled by dew, and shall have placed on it a man of a hundred years; shut and secure the door lest dust or wind should reach them. Then in the time of 180 days send them away to their homes. I say that man shall not cease to eat of the fruit of that tree to the perfection of the number [of the days] until the old man shall become young. O what marvellous natures, which have transformed the soul of that old man into a juvenile body, and the father is made into the son! Blessed be thou, O most excellent God![28]

In this quotation the tree is the *prima materia* placed in its house, or vessel, and watered with dew. The fruit of the tree is perfection and the tree itself is the Stone; the *prima materia* transformed. The old man transformed into a youth is of course a symbol of immortality and rejuvenation, but he is also an alchemical motif representing the purification of the old and corrupted man into a new and glorified form. It may also refer to the transformation of the physical body. This quotation is a good example of how the image of the tree reflected the power of the Stone and the processes related to its creation.

In the encounter between an alchemist and a nymph, which I related in chapter 2, the alchemist is surprised when "it seemed to me that the tree at the foot of which I was sitting suddenly cracked, which caused me to turn my head, and I perceived a nymph, an image of beauty, emerging from the tree."[29]

The nymph of great beauty was Sophia, and in symbolic logic she and the tree are one. The transparency of her clothes refers to the symbol of nudity that in alchemy means a revealed and central truth. Therefore her appearance means that she is revealing herself as she truly is, and in her statement to the alchemists she declares that she is celestial, an emanation from the pole star. She animates everything and is the astral spirit; she gives life to everything and she knows everything. What better way for Sophia to describe herself? She is the life force in all things and knows all things. Remove this life force for an instant and all things die. She is celestial, meaning that she is the spiritual power, and yet she lives in a tree and is the giver of life to all material things—in fact, the giver of life to all things spiritual, as well. The tree is a symbol of the feminine, but here the tree is also the world tree in which Sophia resides, and which she is. If the tree refers to process of individuation, then Sophia is the power that animates that process.

The reference to the pole star is quite interesting. The pole and the pole star related to it symbolize a fixed point, or the center around which the hub of the cosmic wheel rotates. Interestingly enough, the world tree joins the terrestrial to the celestial pole, thus joining the center of the earth to the center of heaven. Sophia links heaven and earth and is the center of both realms. The Philosopher's Stone is also often the center of the centers.[30] In my earlier books I described the essence of ally work as being the union of the human center—the self—with a psychoidal center, the center of God as it were, through the mediation of the ally. Sophia plays the same role as the ally, and is the feminine form of that which unites all of life around the common center, creating the harmony of the *unus mundus*.

In the *Aurora*, when Thomas states that Sophia is the world tree, he is referring to her qualities of animating all of life, knowing all of life, and being the astral, celestial force that is the soul of all existence. One who loves Sophia loves all of that. Furthermore, to have the tree is to possess the Philosopher's Stone and the power of rejuvenation and purification. Imagine for a moment that you are Thomas and that you see before you a numinous feminine being who feels to you as if she were the very essence of life itself. In her loving glance you see the wisdom of the ages, and in her touch you experience the echo of immortality. Is it any wonder that Thomas is so ecstatic?

The Symbolism of Fire

The next image of note in the *Aurora* occurs a few pages later when Thomas discusses the sacred nature of the science that Sophia teaches—alchemy. He writes that anyone who has found this science can live for a thousand years and never lack; moreover such a person could feed seven thousand men at the same time. The Stone is thus a never-ending source of food that one simply cannot exhaust. In this regard, it is similar to both the Holy Grail and the Tao, both of which create unceasingly. In this infinite capacity to create, the Stone is likened to fire.

Thomas quotes Senior, the Western name for a most respected Arabian alchemist Mohammad ibn Umail, who says that the Stone is like fire. While Aristotle wrote that the size and growth of all things is limited, fire, in contrast, grows without end so long as it is fed. Sophia teaches the wisdom of the Stone, which, like fire and Sophia herself, grows without limits. Von Franz comments that this symbol reveals Sophia as a universal rather than a personal soul. As a universal soul, once more related to the idea of the *anima mundi*, she "can bestow unending life without ever exhausting herself. . . . Her action . . . is capable of infinite extension. She gives the prime impulse toward all being and all knowing in their endlessly diverse forms, and as an inexhaustible vitalizing principle her range of action is unlimited."[31]

Like fire, Sophia is a boundless source of life and wisdom. This is the second time that Sophia has been likened to fire, for as *anima mundi*, she was associated with light and fire.

Fire, like light, is an essential concept in alchemy. It is used to cook the ingredients in the retort, and is thus an agent of transformation. Yet fire can also be the enemy of the Stone, for the Stone must be strong enough not to melt in the fire, or it will never form with sufficient power to transform other metals. Like the salamander, the Stone is a creature thought to live in the fire, so that when the alchemist reached the stage that the Stone could live in the fire he called it his salamander.

Fire has even greater significance when one is considering the psychoid and its nature, for fire is a power or force that connects inner and outer, spirit and matter. As one modern writer put it:

> The alchemists believed that the driving force behind the evolution of matter, the connection between mental and physical reality, was Fire. They spent an inordinate amount of time thinking and writing about fire and concluded that it existed on all levels of reality— from the grossest expression of the One Thing in ordinary matter to the most subtle and luminous One Mind.[32]

The alchemists called the fire that was spirit and yet capable of influencing matter their "secret fire." The secret fire could reduce all metals to their primal condition, and so was the key to the discovery of the *prima materia*:

> Our Philosophical mercurial water [secret Fire] is the Key whereby all coagulated, fixed and unfixed metallic and mineral bodies are radically and physically dissolved and reduced into their first principle . . .[33]

This fire is supernatural and even divine[34] and it governs the whole work of alchemy, for there is nothing that the alchemist can add to it.[35] It is also known as the fire of Wisdom, which is no accident considering Sophia's relationship to fire.

According to *The Golden Chain of Homerus*, there are three levels of the secret fire or spirit:

> (a) we say in its first most Universal state it is perfectly invisible and immaterial.
> (b) In its second state of manifestation it is visible in Light, but remains cold and immaterial.
> (c) In its third state of Heat and burning fire it is visible, hot or burning, and becomes somewhat material as it occupies Room or Space whilst in this State.[36]

Of essential importance is the statement that in its pure form fire is immaterial and invisible and then, proceeding through the second stage as light, it becomes burning and visible and "somewhat" material. Fire thus begins as pure spirit and moves into the psychoid realm becoming somewhat material, but still spirit, and thus is able to influence and transform material substances while remaining both spirit and matter. The same author later informs us that all of life derives from this fire that is always in motion and never ceases its creative activity. That such an idea contradicts the Christian view of creation occurring at one specific time does not often occur to the alchemists. Fire, though said to derive from God, is divine in itself and has the power to move from a purely spiritual to a psychoidal state, while it never ceases creating. This description brings us back to the statement in the *Aurora* that one who has this science has that which knows no limits and grows forever.

Some alchemists say that fire does not only produce the *prima materia* but is in fact the *prima materia*. Moreover, since it is the first matter, fire is the Stone itself. One writer states, "let the Students in Philosophy know that from that first Sulphur, a second is generated which may be multiplied ad infinitum: let the wise man, after he hath got the everlasting mineral of that Heavenly Fire, keep it diligently."[37] Notice that the Heavenly Fire is an everlasting mineral; that is, it has become material.

Fire is a celestial spirit, a force or power that can incarnate as matter and, as it does, gains the capacity to transform matter and in fact becomes the Philosopher's Stone with all of its power to purify, transmute, and enlighten. Fire incarnate is the psychoidal Stone and is a source of infinite growth and sustenance that never exhausts itself. As such, fire is one of the greatest mysteries of alchemy. Nor is there any doubt that this fire was related to the feminine being we know as Sophia:

> Moreover, they affirme her to be of that nature that no fire can destroy her, which of all other descriptions is most true, for shee is fire her self, having in her a portion of the universal fire of nature and a secret celestial spirit, which spirit is animated and quickened by God himself, wherefore also they call her their most blessed stone. Lastly, they say shee is a middle nature between thick and thin, neither altogether earthy nor altogether fiere, but a mean aereal substance—to bee found everywhere, and every time of the year.[38]

Fire is a "she" and she is of a middle nature, once more pointing to her nature as a psychoidal force. Sophia is the divine fire that can join matter and spirit together within itself. I cannot, no more than the alchemist could, define what this fire is but, like the alchemist, I have witnessed its being and power. As a purely spiritual force it is invisible and unknowable, but when it manifests as light it begins its journey into the material world with which it then unites. Therefore the inner alchemist must seek the vision of this fire, which is felt and perceived as a dynamic and formless but visible vibration or energetic motion. As it becomes more fixed and "material" it takes on a more fixed character and is felt to gain in substance and power. It becomes more accessible to the eye of the alchemist and can be worked with, though it never takes on pure material form. So powerful is the force that it generates that it can be dangerous to the unprepared. Yet the alchemist of the psychoid need not work within its formless and energetic state alone, for like all forces of the psychoid, it is at the same time an entity; a personification. Of course, this force is personified as Sophia and she is this force. If we were to attempt psychoidal alchemy without knowing the beings that stand behind the force it is unlikely that we would accomplish much, and at worst unlikely that we would endure without some form of injury. Such forces are not for the ego, not even the individuated ego, to handle. It can, however, relate to them and such a relationship is possible because they are entities as well as powers.

Sophia is the entity that ceaselessly generates power and wisdom, and in her universal state she is the driving force of nature. If one relates to her, and witnesses her descent into matter, one helps her become the Philosopher's Stone. At that point, she is no longer a universal undifferentiated power, but a concentrated, single, and unique one that is wed to a specific individual. The role of the alchemist is to perceive this process and thereby make it more real. What we see in the psychoid takes on greater substance and reality, and thus we are the instruments through which Sophia becomes real, and as she becomes real, she becomes the feminine aspect of the Philosopher's Stone.

Some believe that many alchemists do not look for the spirit to descend from above, but seek to liberate it from within matter itself. In fact, these are the two central paradigms of psychoidal alchemy—spirit can become matter by descent, or spirit can be liberated from matter by first ascending, only to descend into purified matter. The concept of fire may be found in both paradigms. For example, Thomas Vaughan wrote that the philosophers "saw that the life of all things here below was a thick fire, or fire imprisoned and incorporated in a certain incombustible, aereaal moysture."[39] They found, moreover, that this moisture was originally derived from heaven. In other words, fire is trapped in matter and must be released, but originally it came from above. There are a number of ways that the alchemists combine the notion of the descent of spirit and the liberation of spirit, but the essential point is that spirit becomes matter and can help matter become spirit. The secret fire is not physical fire, but a psychoidal fire that is the power of transformation incarnate.

Sophia and the Flowing of Spirit

In the conclusion of chapter one of the *Aurora*, Thomas continues to bewilder us. He makes two very significant points in the same paragraph, once more paraphrasing biblical statements about Sophia and quoting other alchemists. He quotes Senior to the effect that the wise man understands Sophia when he has been enlightened by the study of books, especially hidden or occult books. Apparently as a result of this understanding, "every spirit bursteth into flood and followeth its desire."[40] In relation to this statement, Thomas references Senior, who wrote, "It [the tincture] was hidden, lest every spirit should recognize its desire; [for then] it flows, as the seers would say."[41] The mention of the tincture is confusing, and it is helpful to consult von Franz at this point.

She argues, with good reason, that Senior is saying that with enlightenment comes the ability on the part of the human being to release spirits and so aid the tincture. The Arab alchemists defined the tincture as Wisdom, and that which can change things from their potential to their actual state. "According to the philosophical thinking of the Arabs, this would be the creative essence of God and the soul, which, Senior says, becomes 'free'— active—only when the alchemist has 'cleared' his thought by subtle meditation."[42] As she points out, this would make the alchemist equally endowed with creative power which, for the Christian, is usually the possession of God alone. She goes into a lengthy discussion of this idea which the interested reader may find in her commentary.

Thomas is saying that Wisdom helps the alchemist to find the path to the goal, but that the understanding of the wise man helps Wisdom as well. This becomes clearer later in the paragraph when he says that "to meditate upon her is a most natural and subtle undersanding which bringeth her to perfection."[43] In short, the alchemist serves to perfect Wisdom by letting the spirits flow. This statement refers to the all-important alchemical motif that the universe is far from perfection, and requires the work of the alchemist to reach it. No one will ever stumble upon the Philosopher's Stone existing in nature; the human operator must create it. In like fashion, Wisdom is imperfect without the meditation and subtle understanding of the alchemist. This is a particularly alchemical concept dating back to Gnostic origins. The alchemist through his meditation can redeem the fallen Sophia. From the perspective of psychoidal alchemy, the powerful and numinous figure Sophia is incomplete and unfulfilled in some way that only the alchemist may redress. This is a relational point of view, for as Sophia helps the alchemist, the alchemist helps her. As I have indicated, the alchemist may be either male or female, for either may enter into this relationship of redemption with Sophia. Both need Sophia for their own fulfillment. But what could Sophia need?

We have seen already that she is cast into the street and ignored by most people and we may imagine that she suffers from this neglect. Paying attention to her through meditation corrects this neglect and eases the suffering caused by it. We may imagine that the divine world and its expressions neither care for nor need our attention, but such is certainly not the case. The forces of the divine need to be known, to be seen as living entities. They need relationship, for without it they may neither grow nor transform, and for whatever reason, they desire transformation very much. The first redemption of Sophia comes in simply meditating on her.

According to Thomas and Senior, the act of meditation confers on the alchemists understanding, and this understanding releases the creative power of Sophia—it lets the spirits flow. In her interpretation of this text, von Franz seems to be saying that the spirit of the alchemist may flow and his understanding be made perfect, that the act of transformation occurs only within the alchemist. I believe that Thomas is talking about helping Wisdom reach perfection and allowing spirits outside of himself to flow freely. From the psychoidal perspective, the spirits that need to flow would be psychoidal energies that are tied up or blocked when Wisdom is unconscious, or out of relationship. By entering into relationship with her, by bringing her to perfection, the alchemist liberates all of her powers. We are not talking about the soul of a human being, but about spirits that are forces in alchemy capable of impacting physical and psychic realities. Figure 8 on page 63 shows the spirits flowing out of the *prima materia.*

The distinction between body, soul, and spirit is a very difficult one to make, for there is much contradiction in the alchemical literature. I shall discuss each of these in turn, for the subsequent chapters of the *Aurora* treat them one by one. But it would be a mistake to confuse soul and spirit in understanding this last paragraph of chapter one. For the moment, let us say that spirit refers to nonhuman and often impersonal forces that are often found outside the alchemist's psyche. This is not simply projection; it is the recognition of powers outside the human being. Understanding

Figure 8. Spirits flowing from the prima materia.

Wisdom and some of her subtleties allows these spiritual forces to flow freely and to follow their desire. What is their desire? This, too, is a very complicated question, but it is often argued that love and the sympathy between things is the basis of alchemy and magic as well. The symbolism of love, marriage, and sexual union fills the literature and emblems of alchemy, and the notion that love between things makes the work possible is quite common.

Edward Kelly quotes Avicenna as saying that one must "purify husband and wife separately, in order that they may unite more intimately; for if you do not purify them, they cannot love each other."[44] Once purified, the natural desire of the spirits carries them into union with each other, and into a harmonious relationship among themselves. This is reminiscent of the Kabbalistic idea that the Sephiroth of the divine Tree seek union with each other, a union made possible by the actions of human beings. The spirits must be purified first, as Avicenna states, or the desire that they follow is not union or love, but whatever their nature dictates. Unpurified, a war-like spirit moves toward war, and a rapacious spirit preys on the weak. Psychoidal alchemy, through meditation and direct experience of such spirits, purifies them and allows them to follow the direction laid down by

Wisdom, which is toward harmony and union. In this sense, Thomas says that through alchemy every spirit follows its desire and Wisdom reaches its own perfection. The perfection of Wisdom is her wedding with the masculine side of God and the union of all spirits around a common center. Not only does Wisdom guide all spirits to union through the help of the alchemist, she reaches this union herself.

It is easy to say that Wisdom attains perfection through the meditation of the alchemist, but the exact nature of this meditation is not yet clear. Not all meditation is alchemical in character. The beginning of this work, as set forth by Thomas, is to seek, for those that seek Wisdom shall find her. To seek Wisdom is to earnestly enter the meditative state with one intent and one focus: Sophia herself. It is to form the image of this most beautiful of feminine beings and hold that image consistently until the meditator feels him- or herself in the presence of a being who is external, feminine in nature, loving in touch, beautiful in aspect, whose very words light the spark of understanding in the mind.

CHAPTER 4

WHAT WISDOM IS:
SOPHIA'S ROLE IN ALCHEMY

n the next few chapters of the *Aurora Consurgens*, before we reach the first of the parables that describe the actual processes of psychoidal alchemy, Thomas gives more information about Sophia and her place in alchemy. Some of this is repetitive, but important enough for Thomas to repeat and for me to comment on. He begins by saying that if you delight in the thrones of kings and wish to reign forever, then love the light of science; that is, alchemy. The secrets of alchemy make one a king, and not only a king, but also an immortal who lives and reigns forever. The science of alchemy that Thomas teaches, though it is concerned with the secrets of nature, is obviously about the great mysteries, those of life, death, and immortality. As Thomas says, alchemy is a "divine matter" and most alchemists agreed with him. He also points out that the secrets of alchemy are hidden in parables and enigmas, which only a wise man may explain. Thomas is himself such a wise man and he agrees to lay bare the whole secret of the science. He goes on to say that Wisdom is an infinite treasure to all men, and then compares her to the Stone, quoting Senior as saying that there is a stone which "after God hath man no better thing."[1] There is no question that in this short chapter Thomas is equating Wisdom with the Stone, and both with God, or the thing nearest to God. Since the title of the chapter is "What Wisdom Is" I think von Franz is wrong in assuming it is entirely about alchemy. Rather, Thomas is telling us what he believes Wisdom to be: a divine being of some kind, second only to God, the Philosopher's Stone itself, and the treasure that can banish even death. She is sacred and her science, alchemy, is sacred as well; for this reason the philosophers (alchemists) veiled this truth with allegories. Thomas has promised to reveal what Wisdom is, and reveal her worth and her divinity.

In the third chapter of the Aurora, Thomas aims his scorn at any who deny the validity of alchemy. Only fools can refuse its validity, for they do not know what it truly is. This whole section is of little importance, being a rather typical alchemical attack on skeptics and a reminder that pearls are not to be cast before swine. Wisdom is far away from those who mock her or her science.

Thomas next discusses the four reasons he named his book *Aurora Consurgens*, which means "the rising dawn." First, those who succeed in the work discover a golden end, a reference to the gold created by the alchemical opus. Second, just as dawn is midway between night and day, alchemy begets the colors red and yellow which are midway between white and black. The reference to black is to the beginning of the work, which is the time of death and decay known as the *nigredo* or *mortificatio*, and white in this case probably refers to the goal of the work, which stands in opposition to black. Third, those who succeed in the work are like those who labor through the night—they find comfort and rest in the light of the dawning day. As day approaches, "all evil odours and vapours that infect the mind of the laborant fade away and weaken."[2] This is more interesting, for it suggests the psychological effect of succeeding at the alchemical work. All the dark feelings and despairing thoughts disappear when the Stone is attained, and the mind finds rest and joy. This is but a hint at the profound psychological transformation that occurs when the Stone comes into being, and is a reminder that the alchemist's psyche is completely involved in the work on the Stone. It is also a reference once more to the *nigredo*, a process that occurs not only to the material substance, but also takes place in the mind of the alchemist. Finally, and seemingly repeating himself, Thomas states that with dawn all darkness ends and the night is put to flight. Furthermore, "night shall be light as the day in its pleasures."[3] The reference here is quite remarkable, for it is similar to the Roman Missal for the evening of Easter: "O truly blessed night, which alone didst merit to know the time and the hour wherein Christ rose from the dead! This is that night, whereof it is written: And the night shall be light as the day: and night shall be my light in my pleasures."[4]

The origin of the quote from the Easter service is Proverbs, but it is surely no accident that this passage is quoted in the *Aurora* at this point. Day putting night to flight is the conquest of death, for as Jesus rose from the dead at Easter so, too, shall the alchemist rise from the dead when the Stone is created. Thomas may have meant this figuratively; that the alchemist would be reborn in the knowledge of the Stone, but the quest for immortality has always been part of alchemy. Though the Western Christian alchemist could not speak of this frequently for it was heresy to do so, the Chinese alchemists had no qualms about seeking immortality and the accompanying subtle body in which to spend eternity. Recall in the previous section that Thomas speaks openly of reigning forever, so that the reference at this point seems likely to be immortality. When one creates the Stone, when one transforms Wisdom into the Stone and brings her to perfection, one gains immortality and this immortality is symbolized by the rising of the sun at dawn, which ends all darkness.

The theme of immortality also appears in chapter five of the *Aurora*, which opens once more with an attack on the foolish that despise Wisdom. Thomas also reiterates that the wise men speak in parables when talking of the great work, and yet he who understands these riddles will grow wiser and understand, and by understanding he will lay hold upon Wisdom. She is the Queen of the south who, coming to learn from Solomon, received power, honor, and dominion, "bearing upon her head the crown of the kingdom shining with the rays of twelve stars, prepared as a bride adorned for her husband, and having on her garments written in golden letters in Greek, in barbarian <Arabic> script and in Latin: Reigning I will reign, and my kingdom shall have no end for all them that find me and subtly and ingeniously and constantly seek me out."[5]

We are reminded in this chapter of the earlier reference to the south wind, for the Queen is of the south, a reference to the Queen of Sheba, who visited Solomon, and was considered to be a great alchemist. The Queen of the south, the goddess Sophia, was honored greatly for her own wisdom. Thomas depicts her with the crown of the kingdom shining with the rays of twelve stars. The reference to the kingdom takes us back to the earlier statement that one who desires thrones may reign forever, so it is another reference to the kingdom of alchemy and its gift of immortality. Von Franz reveals the connection between this image and the woman of the apocalypse who wore twelve stars. Following her amplifications from mostly theological sources, von Franz concludes that this woman stands for "a self-subsistent power . . . a power of illumination pervading nature."[6] She relates her, of course, to Sophia.

The crown in alchemy is an image of divinity and enlightenment. Holmyard speaks of the golden crown that represents the achievement of the great work.[7] Jung speaks of the crown signifying "kingly totality; it stands for unity. . . . This reminds us of the seven—or twelve-rayed crown of light which the Agathodaimon serpent wears on Gnostic gems, and also of the crown of Wisdom in the Aurora Consurgens."[8] The Agathodaimon is a figure that appears in the writings of the early alchemist Zosimos and represents both a wise teacher and the *prima materia* itself, which is subjected to horrible torments in its transformative process.[9] Sophia and the Agathodaimon wear the same crown and both are the primal force that the alchemist transforms.

In *The Glory of the World*, the Stone is crowned with light.[10] Most often, as in this case, the crown is a symbol of the completion of the work, though almost every metal appears crowned in one alchemical text or another. The crown emitting light is especially related to the achievement of the work. Jung discusses the crown of light as it appears in the *Aurelia Occulta*, a late medieval alchemical text. It contains the figure of a shining man, wearing a crown of stars, who is a guide for the alchemist, and yet, according to Jung, is also an image for the second Adam, a divine figure parallel to Christ.[11]

The crown of stars that Sophia wears is a cosmic image, marking its bearer as a goddess. It also indicates that she is not only a wisdom figure and a guide, but also the personification of the original matter that the alchemist transforms. Sophia thus appears once more as the embodiment of a cosmic force that still lacks completion and must undergo its own process of transformation.

Recall that the crown worn by the Queen of the south bears an inscription in three languages. This is no doubt a reference to the extremely important number three in alchemy, as for example in the three kingdoms the Stone rules: animal, vegetable, and mineral. It may be a reference to the triad of spirit, soul, and body as well, and certainly indicates that Sophia rules the whole world. It is noteworthy that Greek, Arabic, and Latin are the main languages of Western alchemy, so the inscription indicates she is also the queen of the alchemists wherever they worked. The inscription also points to the theme of immortality, for it says that the queen reigns now and will reign forever and welcomes into her kingdom those with the wisdom to discover her.

Alchemy is not only a mystery religion; it is a Gnostic philosophy as well. We cannot succeed in alchemy without knowledge, both of a scholarly and Gnostic kind. We must read, decipher, and study the allegories and mysteries of the philosophers, or we shall never find Sophia. But intellectual understanding alone never suffices, for without illumination the parables remain completely obscure. We need wisdom to find Wisdom. I emphasize this because the Gnostic nature of study and knowledge is often ignored today, where gnosis is seen as a freely-given gift of the self or of the gods.

But in my experience it almost never comes without great individual effort, an effort that includes thinking as well as feeling, and that necessitates extended study. If we wish success in alchemy at whatever level—physical, inner, or psychoidal—we must study and read and make a total effort to understand. After so much effort, if the alchemist is lucky, gnosis occurs. I am often amazed by the attitude of entitlement of many people seeking individuation and visionary insight. They often grow angry and frustrated if no results are immediately forthcoming. It is the task of a lifetime to gain a glimpse of Sophia's kingdom, which she promises only to those "that find me and subtly and ingeniously and constantly seek me out."[12]

There is one last image in chapter five of the *Aurora* worth noting. Sophia is prepared as a bride adorned for her husband. All images related to marriage portray the *coniunctio*, the union that leads to the creation of the Stone and of the Self. Though Thomas does not reveal whom Sophia is to marry, we may safely assume that she has two grooms. Von Franz believes Thomas is the groom, and this is certainly part of the truth. As we have seen, Sophia comes as a lover to the alchemists, some of whom fondly look forward to union with her in the life to come. By participating in the divine mysteries represented by the *coniunctio*, the alchemist, male or female, gains the opportunity to unite with Sophia. To marry a psychoidal figure means to relate to them so deeply that our soul is permanently joined with it. The psyche receives an influx of such a figure's teachings and energies and experiences a transformation. The psychoidal figure, though never loosing its autonomy, becomes more personally connected to us and is "humanized" by the relationship. Wisdom does not cease to be Wisdom, but to a degree, it becomes our beloved Wisdom, more personal and particular to us.

At the same time, there is an even deeper wedding that occurs, for Sophia marries her divine partner. Although the *Aurora* does not specify this partner, it is presented as God in the text, and if we bear in mind the concept of the Names, we see that two Names are being joined in the *coniunctio*, establishing a new Name and a new harmony between the two previously separated Names. Since all the Names belong to the One Thing, we can say that there is a transformation occurring within the godhead as two aspects of its manifestation are joined in balance and harmony. This is a main theme of the Kabbalah in which Love and Power wed, or, alternatively, the indwelling feminine presence of God marries the masculine focus of the divine powers: the *Shekinah* weds *Yesod* or *Tifereth*. In either case, the Kabbalist views these weddings as creating a new harmony within the manifested God, and new blessings for the world. Thus, Sophia is preparing for the last stage of the work, when she is to marry a masculine Name and form a union with it, thus creating a whole new depth of the divinity. The union of the masculine and feminine sides of the Divine, the marriage of Sophia, is the culmination of the *Aurora* and indeed of psychoidal alchemy. She is prepared at this point, but she is not yet a bride, for the work that will make her so is yet to come. It is perhaps for this reason that the next chapter of the *Aurora* begins the description of the actual processes Sophia must undergo in order to reach the final stage of union.

CHAPTER 5

OF THE BLACK EARTH

hapters six through twelve of the *Aurora Consurgens* present seven alchemical parables that describe Sophia's transformation. With the first parable of the Black Earth, the actual process of transformation begins. Though Thomas continues to quote the Bible, he now begins to speak of alchemy and its operations, especially the transformations of body, soul, and spirit. An important problem immediately presents itself that must be addressed before we can try to make sense of what follows. Who is transforming? The text can be quite confusing throughout its remaining chapters. I agree with von Franz in her statement that:

> In the passages that follow it is not always clear who is actually speaking. Sometimes it seems to be the author or aritfex, sometimes the arcane substance or its indwelling spirit; and often it cannot be made out whether this is its masculine or its feminine personification (sponsus or sponsa). One gets the impression that the author, giving free rein to his "true imagination" has sometimes let the voices of the unconscious speak directly, and that he himself is only occasionally taking part in the conversation with his ego-consciousness.[1]

Thomas is witnessing a process of transformation occurring within the indwelling spirit of the arcane substance, which is Sophia. At times, a masculine voice speaks and at times a feminine voice, so we must assume that the two aspects of the Stone are in dialogue, and are both experiencing transformation. The indwelling spirit of the arcane substance or the divine principle in its masculine aspect is the masculine Name I refer to as God. The indwelling spirit in its feminine aspect is Sophia. In their dialogue they create their own transformation and their own union. The ego, as witness, also transforms, but Thomas is not only describing his own transformational processes but also that of the Stone, or the indwelling or psychoidal God. For God to make itself known and to present itself for transformation, it must take on form, a form that has substance and materiality. Thus God enters the psychoid world in order to be known by the alchemist and in order to be transformed. The alchemist watches and attends, and it is this attention that helps to create the divine transformation.

There are many levels of alchemy. On one level, it is the human being who transforms, and all the processes of alchemy of this type concern his or her soul and body. At another level, when we have "taken" a psychoidal force as our subject, the transformation concerns not the human soul or body but that of the psychoidal entity. When Thomas writes of the body transforming and gaining immortality, he refers only indirectly to his human body. More directly, he is describing the transformation of the *prima materia* that we have seen to be Sophia. In what follows, therefore, Sophia or her spouse does most of the talking. Thomas allows them to speak through his voice by using "true imagination," or what we have called the Gnostic imagination.

This insight is crucial for the interpretation of this text on the psychoid level. It is hard enough for people to imagine the reality of psychoidal beings; it is still harder to imagine that they seek transformation. Perhaps harder still is the concept that they have body, soul, and spirit. Yet the alchemists repeatedly declare that the Stone is like a human being in having these three components. For example, one writer states that, "Our Stone has body, soul, and spirit, the imperfect body is the body, the ferment the soul, and the water the spirit."[2] In other words, the *prima materia* and the Stone possess body, soul, and spirit, and these components must each be altered and recombined to create the transformation of the *prima materia* into the Stone.

In the subsequent chapters of the *Aurora*, the processes of changing body, soul, and spirit are presented. Keep in mind that when we speak of "body," we are not speaking of the human body or even a physical body, but a psychoidal body in which the spirit has incarnated. Recall that the spirit cannot be known until it takes on form or body. Since in our text Sophia is the Stone, it is Sophia's body, soul and spirit that undergo change. I shall explain what such changes consist of as we explore the *Aurora*.

It is difficult, even under the best of circumstances, for a modern Westerner to relate to alchemical imagery. It is a great help to be able to take an alchemical image and illustrate how a person might experience that image in his or her own psychological life. Most books of inner alchemy do just that, and I tried in *Jung and the Alchemical Imagination* to illustrate the experiences of the individual that paralleled alchemical processes. But now I am writing of psychoidal entities and the changes that they undergo. You may have trouble relating this to your own experience, and for good reason, since I am no longer speaking of changes that you, as an individual, undergo. Nevertheless, the human being is the essential witness to psychoidal transformation. Such transformation cannot occur without this witnessing. The very act of witnessing transforms the human observer as well. Such experiences are ecstatic in nature and add energy and knowledge to the human self, but they are not designed primarily for human transformation. The human being must at some time come to realize that spiritual growth necessarily carries him or her beyond normal human development. Though it goes against the grain, he or she must admit that spiritual work concerns the Other just as much as, or even more so, than it does his or her soul. In many ways, spiritual and psychological work on the individual is preparation for the deeper work of transforming God.

There is an alchemical axiom that the operator experiences exactly what the substance operated upon experiences. In this sense, Thomas hopes for his own immorality if Sophia achieves union with God. The human observer does participate in the process by witnessing, and does share in the transformations that follow. But these transformations concern the divine primarily, and it is as they concern the divine that Thomas describes them.

We can experience the psychoidal events I shall discuss by observing them. When I write about Sophia's transformation I shall make every attempt to also describe how the human eyewitness might perceive and feel it, in order to make these events more comprehensible. But for the sake of clarity let me reiterate that when Thomas talks of body, soul, and spirit he is letting his "true imagination" operate and allowing Sophia, and sometimes her partner, to speak of their own experiences through him. He is the witness.

Anyone who experiences the psychoid knows that such an experience creates altered states of consciousness as well as profound feelings. All such experiences are *felt experiences,* and therefore when we witness an alteration in the nature of the psychoidal figure we undergo intense, often ecstatic, feelings. "Witness" may sound like a bland word, but one who beholds the psychoid operations is profoundly affected. Thomas is profoundly touched by what he sees. Yet he is describing not what he himself has undergone, but what Sophia has. It is important to keep this distinction in mind, or the interpretations presented in the following pages will be confusing and mis-leading.

SOPHIA'S PLEA

The *Aurora's* "Parable of the Black Earth" is quite strange in the juxtaposi-tion of ideas and the confusion about who is speaking. It seems at first as if Thomas were speaking, but only by assuming that Thomas's voice is Sophia's does a consistent interpretation emerge and the strangeness of the text disappear. Many times when encountering a psychoidal figure we lend our mind and our voice to it and it speaks through us. This is the origin of the much-abused word "channeling" and is a technique as old as shaman-ism. I myself have experienced the autonomy of the voice of a psychoidal figure in which it has only been necessary to record what the other says. It is not even necessary to imagine it in the normal sense, for the psychoidal figure speaks loudly and clearly. Sophia speaks in this way in the first para-ble of the black earth.

She begins by saying that she saw from afar "a great cloud looming black over the whole earth, which had absorbed the earth and covered my soul, <because> the waters had come in even unto her, wherefore they were putrefied and corrupted before the face of the lower hell and the shadow of death, . . . there is no health in my flesh and all my bones are troubled . . . who is the man that liveth, knowing and undersanding, delivering my soul from the hand of hell?"[3]

Black is the color of the *nigredo*, often the first stage in the alchemical work. It is the juncture at which the original substance dies so that a process of transformation may begin through which it is brought back to life in a new, glorified condition. I have argued all along that Sophia is the original substance with which Thomas is operating. In this section, she begins the suffering of hell and her own death in order to reach a new level of existence.

Yet, what can it mean for a psychoidal figure to die and be reborn? All psychoidal figures are not only capable of transformation—they seek it. Though a figure like Sophia is a divinity, she is imperfect and incomplete. This imperfection lies not in her nature or in her quality, but in her alive-ness and, as it were, in her quantity. She exists in and of herself and is Wisdom and the living force behind all life. Yet, she is weak and unfulfilled compared to what she could be. Recall the notion of the fallen or lower Sophia trapped in matter, and unable to redeem either herself or creation. Recall the alchemist's idea that the secret fire lies dormant in matter, incapable of operating its magical powers without the help of the alchemist. These ideas, and others like them, point to the fact that Sophia is held in thrall, not by physical matter, but by her own imperfect state. She operates at a fraction of the power and capacity potentially available to her.

Psychoidal alchemy begins with the presumption that psychoidal beings exist apart from the human psyche and, though there are many kinds of such beings, it is primarily concerned with divine powers and forces. It also presumes that these forces and powers are blocked and hindered by their own natural state that is imperfect and in some way contaminated. It concludes that it can transform these powers, awakening them to their full potential and then uniting them to their common center. The alchemist at the psychoid level must operate with these assumptions and then experience them. He or she does so by first learning to perceive them, and then witnessing their being, power, and activity. In so doing, the alchemist sets up a relationship with the psychoidal figure with which he or she is working. In almost every case I have witnessed it takes but a short time for the psychoidal figure to state that it needs help and that it is trapped. At this point, the alchemist begins his or her work in earnest. In the first parable, Sophia describes her hellish condition and asks: Who is the man that can deliver my soul from the hand of hell? The answer is: The alchemist.

Sophia's hell has begun with the appearance of the black cloud and the start of the *nigredo* that affects both her body and soul, but this hell is necessary because of her need for development and transformation.

Since the black cloud is the central figure in this section, it is necessary to ask how the alchemist made use of such an image. The color black is always associated with the *nigredo.* As for the cloud, it appears often in alchemical symbolism. Lyndy Abraham explains that during the stage of the *nigredo* "the 'body' of the metal or Stone is killed and separated from its soul and spirit, a black cloud or shadow is said to be cast over the alchemist and his work."[4] And in the fascinating text of Komarios quoted at length by von Franz in her book on death, the cloud carries the souls of the dead to liberation:

> And the blessed waters flow down to the dead who are lying there, who are bound and oppressed in the gloominess and darkness of the depths of Hades. And how life's curing element enters in and awakens them, so that they revive for their creators. And how the new [fresh] waters into the head of the grave bed and are born in the bed and come forth with the light and the cloud carries them

upward. And the cloud which carries the waters rises up from the
sea. When the adepts see this apparition, they rejoice.[5]

The cloud has to do with the process of sublimation in which the soul and
spirit of the arcane substance is removed from the body. The cloud, like
vapor, rises to the top of the retort. It is believed to carry with it both the
soul and spirit. Most often, this depicts the death of the *prima materia* as
its soul is separated from its body. Sometimes the cloud elevates and liberates the soul from death. Both images apply to the parable, for Sophia is
dying, and is plunged into hell or the underworld like the dead in the
Komarios text, but she will be reborn when soul and spirit are reunited
with her body.

   After complaining of her sickness and descent to hell, Sophia asks who
will save her, and says that the one who "explains me shall have eternal life,
and to him I will give to eat of the tree of life which is in paradise, and to sit
with me on the throne of my kingdom."[6] She goes on to say, in that pecu-
liar litany of the *Aurora*, that he who digs for her as he would for money and
obtains her as treasure, who does not disturb the tears of her eyes or mock
her garments, who neither poisons her food nor defiles her with fornica-
tion; he who does not "violate my whole body which is exceeding delicate
and above all my soul . . . he for whose love I languish, in whose ardour I
melt, in whose odour I live, by whose sweetness I regain my health, from
whose milk I take nourishment, in whose embrace I am made young, from
whose kiss I receive the breath of life, in whose loving embrace my whole
body is lost, to him indeed I will be a father and he shall be to me a son."[7]

   Recall in the previous chapter of the *Aurora* that Thomas spoke of the
enigmas and parables that obscure the truth, and that one must penetrate this
opaqueness to learn the mysteries of alchemy. Sophia promises the gift of
eternal life to the one who understands her and who elucidates her secrets.
This is coupled with the statement that we must dig for her like money; that
is, for one endeavoring to experience Sophia and help her through the process
of transformation, we must "know" and "desire" her.

   The process of knowing combines the pursuit of intellectual understanding by study, reading, reflection, and questioning with gnosis, or the
direct experience of insight that transcends mere intellectual understanding. Yet both gnosis and intellect are necessary in this difficult work. As I
mentioned earlier, many people today hold intellectual understanding in
contempt, and many ask what relevance alchemy has for ordinary life. Why
study such arcane material? What good will it do for my marriage or my

career? How will it help me individuate? There is a phase in the study of alchemy in which it is useful for all the practical issues of life; when it helps a person understand his or her own inner dynamics and the patterns of their life. Yet that is not what Sophia is talking about in this section, nor is it what psychoidal alchemy concerns itself with primarily. Of course, encountering the psychoid has an incredible impact on the psyche, and causes profound changes of all kinds, sometimes beneficial, but not always. Psychoidal alchemy's primary goal is the not the understanding of our own personality nor its application to relationship issues or body symptoms or any such personal concerns. That belongs to the earlier stages of alchemy, when it is the psyche that is the focus of study. Sophia is not asking you to understand her in terms of your life, but to understand her in terms of hers. At a certain moment in the work, we must shift our focus from our own needs and wants to those of the psychoidal figure who is now our *prima materia*. Before, the *prima materia* was ourselves; now it is the Other.

The question still remains: Why should we explain Sophia? Why study her and labor to gain the insight of gnosis? In the first place, she promises immortality to the one who achieves understanding and creates the Stone. But more important is attaining union with Sophia to sit with her on the throne of her kingdom. We seek Sophia herself for her own sake and for the union she promises. Imagine the greed of one digging for money, the hunger for treasure and wealth that drives so many people to work most of their lives. We must feel the same hunger for Sophia. We must feel driven to know her and to explain her, to feel her and savor the love she offers. We must desire this union as one digging for money in the earth, seeking the buried treasure of our hearts.

We study psychoidal alchemy not for the practical results that might be obtained. We do it because we hear Sophia's cry of pain, and we hunger for her love, as the miser hungers for gold or the pilgrim hungers for God. Without this hunger, without this compassion, we cannot come to know her. It is this longing that allows us to study, to meditate on her, and to finally suffer the agony of her agony as she dies and transforms. Without such yearning none could undergo the trials that follow. Do not ask what practical results follow from psychoidal alchemy, do not reduce this work to the limits of your own personal life and its issues. Rather, ask what change in the universe can it create. What power we possess to help the psychoidal spirits transform! That is the goal, and it requires the capacity to transcend our own limits and grasp for a time that our consciousness has a purpose beyond its application in our lives. It is for this reason that so much is promised to those who understand, for understanding requires study, gnosis, and self-sacrifice. We seek the Other out of love and out of the desire to heal her. What happens to us in the process, no matter how profound, must remain secondary.

Such a wide perspective and deep compassion for the psychoidal entity is hard to find. In fact, not only do most people refuse to consider that psychoidal entities exist at all, but should they believe in their reality, they seek only what benefits themselves. The literature of magic and occultism, as well as alchemy is filled with examples of those seeking to control and dominate the spirit. Sophia warns that they who defile her and violate her will not know her. The references to the body and the soul in this passage of the *Aurora* have alchemical meaning, but in psychoidal alchemy all depends on the correct relationship between the alchemist and the psychoidal entity. To defile Sophia's body and soul is to try to use her for our own gain. It is also to ignore her, to live life without wisdom and to live it from the tiny perspective of the ego.

I wonder sometimes, strange as it seems, who defiles Wisdom more: the one who seeks to bend her to personal use, or the one who ignores her completely. To live without Wisdom is to live an illusion, but an illusion that is ultimately destructive not only to the person living it, but to his community and family, and to the universe itself. I had the following dream once:

> I beheld a giant wheel in the sky. It was the wheel of the cosmos and everything that was existed within that wheel. Every person who ever lived and those who had not yet been born were in that wheel and every person had a certain place within it. But in my dream everything was in chaos and nothing was in its proper place. There was a powerful pulsing energy that circled the wheel. As it whirled around the wheel it collided with everything that was out of place, and out of the collision came a blue spark that shot off in all directions. I knew in the dream that the blue spark was the source of all evil and suffering. Suddenly I realized where my spot was on the wheel and I entered it. As I did so, everything else in the wheel entered their proper niches. As the energy circulated it hit nothing because everything was in its proper place and instead of blue sparks, a golden light radiated within the wheel.

Sophia shows us where our spot is, where we belong, and what our path is and must be. Knowing Sophia means knowing who and what we are. If we know Sophia, we put the universe in order, at least to the limited extent that we are able. Putting the universe in order ends evil, which emerges from our ignorance and our being out of place. To defile the pure body and soul of Sophia is to participate in the creation of evil. And no matter who we are and what we do; no matter how good we seem and how hard we try to end suffering, if we remain ignorant of Wisdom, we defile her.

SOPHIA AND THE FILIUS

After making her appeal to us, Sophia moves into expressions of love and all of her statements of endearment refer to alchemy and alchemical processes that we shall examine. First, though, it must be noted that her gender in the *Aurora* text changes from the feminine to the masculine, and she promises to be a father to the one who helps her. I understand this change to indicate the close relationship between Sophia and the masculine side of the Philosopher's Stone. One way to understand this change is by consulting von Franz's interpretation in which she rightly points out that the heavenly being who now appears is the *filius philosophorum*, the personification of the Philosopher's Stone. This masculine being is "the glorified, ultimate manifestation of the *prima materia* and is thus in a mysterious manner identical with Wisdom."[8] On the other hand, we can argue that the two aspects of the Stone, masculine and feminine, talk through Thomas, and both seek redemption.

The *filius* is a psychoidal being that represents the Stone as a living creature with body, soul, and spirit. It is the fullest expression of the Stone as the center of all the worlds and as the incarnation of divinity. It is God who manifests as the *prima materia* and individualizes through the alchemical processes. Giving birth to the *filius* is the ultimate goal of alchemy, and results from the union of the feminine and masculine aspects of the Stone. Hence, I believe that it is the father of the Stone that speaks, rather than the Stone's masculine voice, as von Franz posits. That is, it is not yet the Stone or the ally that is speaking, but the God who, in union with Sophia, will give birth to the ally.

After the shift to the masculine voice, the figure of the dove is introduced, who is called a beloved son covered with gold and silver and "at whose beauty the sun and moon wonder. For he is the privilege of love and the heir, in whom men trust and without whom they can do nothing."[9] This is a typical description of the *filius*. The first masculine figure, the father, is the *prima materia*, or the divinity before its union with Sophia, and the son is the *filius*, the end of the work, the transformed and glorified God who has become unique and individuated.

The passage now turns to a description of the alchemical process, and it seems to be God who continues to talk. He suddenly introduces the image of the seven stars, by which the divine work is wrought. Thomas quotes Senior as saying that after "thou hast made those seven <metals> which thou hast distributed through the seven stars (and hast appointed to the seven stars) <and> hast purged them nine times until they appears as pearls (in likeness)—this is the Whitening."[10]

We suddenly have a whole new cast of characters. As von Franz points out, the central symbol has become a plurality.[11] She takes this in a negative way as a sign of regression, but I prefer to see it in terms of the complications that arise in psychoidal alchemy when we realize that though the ally is the center, there are many other divine, psychoidal forces that play a role. The seven metals are an obvious alchemical image, but they represent the seven stars, which is a reference to astrology[12] and the idea that each metal corresponded to a planet, and each planet was a force that emanated rays or in some other fashion affected life on Earth and the alchemical process. In other words, we have in the reference to the seven stars an allusion to the existence of many other psychoidal forces that can be brought into the alchemical process and in some way united with the *filius*. To pursue the way in which this is done will take us too far afield of our coming to know Sophia. I believe that the *Aurora* suddenly introduces the other stars to demonstrate the multiple nature of the ally or the Stone. The Stone is a unity, a central unifying force into which may be added many other forces. For example, according to *The Emerald Tablet*, "It rises from earth to heaven and comes down again from heaven to earth, and thus acquires the power of the realities above and the realities below. In this way you will acquire the glory of the whole world, and all darkness will leave you."[13] The "it" is the *filius*, which ascends to the higher world of spirit and incorporates the heavenly powers within itself and descends again.

The Stone is a unity within a multiplicity. It multiplies itself by adding spiritual energies that heighten its own power and complexity of being. This process occurs during and after the birthing of the *filius*. In psychoidal alchemy, a psychoidal force or being is the *prima materia*. If it is the ally it will in time become the *filius*. If it is another psychoidal being that represents some aspect of the spirit or the divine, it will become one with the *filius*. And such is the case with Sophia.

Sophia is a psychoidal being in her own right who is beginning her own transformation process. However, she goes through two other transformations as well. She marries her masculine spouse and she gives birth to the *fil-*

ius or Stone. In a typical alchemical paradox, she is the mother of the Stone and yet the Stone itself; at least its feminine side. In this parable of the black earth, Thomas speaks with the voice of Sophia and that of her spouse, and then describes the child of their union. These three are the main components of the alchemical process, but the seven stars reflect all the other powers that can be added to the Stone. These powers are added before and after its birth, but always multiply its power and depth.

After the masculine divine voice introduces the seven planets, he speaks of his "beloved son . . . at whose beauty the sun and moon wonder. For he is the privilege of love and the heir in whom men trust, and without whom they can do nothing."[14] This beautiful son is the Philosopher's Stone, and the sun and moon that wonder at his beauty are his father and mother, the masculine and feminine poles of the godhead. They give birth to the son and they are both parts of the son.

The paradoxical relationship of parents to child is most often expressed in terms of the king and his son. Thomas points out two sources that relate to the father and son image. Petrus Bonus, an alchemist of the 14th century, wrote that on the completion of the work the "begetter and the begotten become altogether one; and old man child, father and son, become altogether one."[15] The *Turba Philosophorum*, an old alchemical text, is also cited, stating that the "old man ceaseth not to eat of the fruits of the tree . . . until that old man become a youth . . . and the father hath become the son."[16] The imagery points to rejuvenation and renewal as the old man becomes the young man. The parallels with the *Aurora* are clear enough, but what is meant by this symbol? That it can have a spiritual and even divine significance is clear. In the quote from Bonus, the first part of the sentence refers to the alchemist of old who "knew also that God was to be made man, because on the last day of this Art, on which is the completion of the work, the begetter and the begotten become altogether one."[17] God the father becomes one with his human son, and the human and the divine are altogether one. This refers to the union of the human Self with the ally (the psychoidal divine Self). In the *Aurora*, it means that the *prima materia*, which is Sophia, becomes one with her child, who is the ally. The ally is her child because the end product of the transformation of the *prima materia* of whatever kind is the Stone. All roads lead to Rome; all transformations lead to the Stone. The Stone, as mentioned, cannot be conceived of as only a simple unity, though it is that, but paradoxically it is the center of a multilayered totality that includes attributes and powers of many kinds. When Sophia becomes the Stone, the Stone becomes Sophia, and gains the wisdom, penetrative and creative powers associated with her. It embraces and becomes one with the feminine, as Sophia becomes one with it.

.   .   .

Sophia enters the underworld and dies by having her body separate from its soul and spirit. She is in the *nigredo* and she complains bitterly of her suffering and asks her lover, the alchemist, to come to her aid and to understand her. The alchemist must next practice his art on Sophia in order to begin the movement from the *nigredo* to the *albedo*, the whitening. This hints at the *coniunctio* and the voice of Sophia's lover appears, describing the love between him and Sophia and praising the fruit of their union, the *filius*. The parable ends with the appearance of the powers that aid in the process of transformation and help bring Sophia back to life. However, Thomas is only pointing at the *albedo*, for the parable is really concerned with the death of Sophia and the operations that the alchemist must perform.

We are now in a position to return to the description of those processes and to amplify them. The black cloud represented the separation of the body and the soul and spirit so that Sophia has died to her former nature. Now she seeks the one who will heal her: her divine lover. She seeks the one "for whose love I languish, in whose ardour I melt, in whose odour I live, by whose sweetness I regain my health, from whose milk I take nourishment, in whose embrace I am made young, from whose kiss I receive the breath of life, in whose loving embrace my whole body is lost."[18] Right at this point in the parable Sophia turns into the groom seeking his bride; and thus her union with the masculine has begun. As we have seen, however, the masculine divinity turns toward his son as well and describes the nature of the son.

The ally is a psychoidal entity capable of infinite transformations and adductions, capable of bringing into itself and ordering all the psychoidal forces of the universe. In this sense, it is the child of them all, for each produces in its turn a new aspect or attribute of the ally. The power that is the *prima materia* does not disappear, but becomes pure and finds its proper place within the wholeness that the ally is.

Sophia must die to her original nature and melt in the union with her lover, so that their power becomes merged in the formation of the son. In order to fully understand this image it is necessary to amplify the very complicated image of the body.

THE BODY

Body, soul, and spirit form one of the most important trinities in alchemy. The *prima materia* and the Stone possess body, soul, and spirit, each of which plays a role in the alchemical enterprise. So closely intertwined are these that we cannot discuss one without involving the other two. For example, the alchemists say that one must make the body spirit and the spirit body, so that the dissolution of the body has a profound impact on the spirit. Nevertheless, to avoid confusion, I shall discuss each of the three in the appropriate place, and discuss their interactions when the *Aurora* describes them.

To begin with the body, it is of course the vessel that contains the soul and the spirit. Without a body the spirit and the soul cannot incarnate in the physical world. The same is true of the psychoid; every psychoidal figure has body, soul, and spirit. The body of the psychoid is also a container, and acts to hold the soul and spirit just as the physical body does. The body is thus first a vessel. As we have seen, the body in which the psychoidal entity incarnates is an image within the Gnostic imagination. The psychoidal body is made of quasi-matter, a more subtle type of matter that is both matter and spirit at the same time, yet it has substance. Jacob Boehme believed that Adam and Eve had bodies before the fall and that all things of a spiritual nature have substance. He followed Paracelsus's lead in calling the Adamic body *limbus*, where limbus is "the universal world, the Four Primal Elements of the World, and of all things, Seed and Matter."[19] There is some evidence that Paracelsus believed that matter was eternal in its own right, and in fact primal matter is of a spiritual nature.

This may become clearer when we consider the second attribute of body—that it is the form of matter. As one alchemist wrote, "all metals [bodies] are compounded of Mercury and Sulphur, Matter and Form."[20] George Ripley equates body and form and states that:

> When the body is from his first form altered,
> A new form is induced immediately.[21]

In this sense, body gives form to spirit and soul. One reason the alchemist wishes to destroy the first body, say of lead, and transmute it into a new body, say of gold, is to give spirit a more perfect form. "Killing" the original body destroys the original form in the hopes of creating a new and more perfect one.

Since body gives form, the psychoidal body gives form to the psychoidal being. A purely spiritual being cannot be known unless it enters the psychoid realm wherein it may encounter a human being. In order to enter the psychoid realm it must put on a body, which means to put on a form. It assumes a shape and a visible aspect that the human may then perceive and to which he or she may relate. It assumes a body that gives best expression to its own nature. Sophia assumes the form of a majestic Queen crowned with power, a goddess of Wisdom.

The alchemical work begins with the destruction of the old body and the old form in order to create a new, purified, and more perfect form. Edward Kelly wrote:

> For as the soul is the bond of the spirit, so the body must also join
> to itself the soul, which can only be after putrefaction; for nothing
> can be improved if its form has not previously been utterly
> destroyed.[22]

It should be clear by now that the body is that which forms matter, and in this form it houses soul and spirit. So linked are these three that the form of the body directly affects soul and spirit, and that to change the body alters both soul and spirit. Thus alchemy seeks to destroy the old form in order to create a higher, purified and spiritualized body. The more refined the body, the more powerfully the spirit works within it. The glorified and highest form of body is the Philosopher's Stone.

At the psychoid level, Sophia joins with God to unite and create the Philosopher's Stone, which is her new body. In her lover's embrace she is made young and at the same time loses her body. As she loses her body, she receives a new one and a better one, for that is the way of alchemy. As I pointed out, the body of the psychoidal figure is the form in which that figure appears in the psychoid. It is hard to imagine how Sophia's original form might be improved upon. There is in fact only one way—she looses her body by becoming one with the ally and sharing the body of the ally, which is the most perfect body of the Stone, in deepest union. She loses her body in her embrace with her lover, who also loses his body. In their deepest union they become the son for as they loose their bodies they form the body of the son.

Many alchemical images depict the union of two beings in one body, such as that shown in figure 9 on page 85, which is often referred to as the *rebis*. Notice that both the masculine and feminine aspects of this creature

Figure 9. The two-headed rebis symbolizes the union of the masculine and feminine as these two sides merge into one being, the filius.

hold two separate crowns, yet wear one shared crown. The crown once more indicates their divinity and the shared crown reveals the depths of their union. They stand upon the monstrous *prima materia*. Also note the two separate heads emerging from the original matter. The *rebis* can thus be the beginning of the work or the completion of the work. At the beginning of the work it is monstrous as shown in the illustration, and the two heads must be separated. But at the end of the work it is glorious and an image for the completion of the work. Their wings reveal their spiritual nature, but they are fully grounded in the earth, for note the crown lying at their feet. The body that unites God and Sophia also grounds them in the subtle earth of the psychoid, giving them form as well as substance.

The *rebis*, with its two heads, indicates the attainment of the ideal union of the masculine and feminine aspects of the Stone. In her dictionary of alchemy, Lyndy Abraham defines *rebis* as "the perfect integration of male and female energies."[23] Hence the image of Sophia losing her body and melting into her lover leads to the creation of the new, third state, that of the son. In this union she finds rebirth and nourishment and in her turn gives her power and essence to the ally.

All these processes occur within the imaginal world witnessed by the alchemist. He beholds the death of Sophia and her lover, as they lose their old imaginal forms to first melt into nothingness. At this point the alchemist cannot witness Sophia as a separate being, for she has merged completely with the masculine side. Out of this merger appears a new image—that of the *filius*. Sophia reappears not as an independent being but as the feminine side of the *filius* and, though nothing of her is lost, she has undergone a metamorphosis and has become part of a larger whole. This creation of the miraculous child, the fruit of the unified divinity, is the redemption of Sophia and of her partner, as well as that of the alchemist, who finds immortality and salvation in the birth of the *filius*.

THE FLOOD OF WATERS:
THE REDEMPTION OF A GODDESS

A lthough the end of the *Aurora*'s first parable of the black earth closed with the description of the last stage of the alchemical work, the section as a whole described the *nigredo*. The death of the body led to the possibility of the formation of a new body, and a union with the ally through the melting of Sophia into her lover. This melting of one body into another often takes place in the *solutio*, the alchemical process in which the body becomes liquid in order to make for a deeper union. The *nigredo*, as the first stage, is now followed by the *solutio*, and so Sophia begins describing the waters that have covered her. But as always, the ecstatic outpourings of Thomas, through whom the powers speak, speed us on to other images.

Sophia, who once more is the speaker in the second parable, begins with the description of the flood by speaking of the time when "the multitude of the sea shall be converted to me and the streams have flowed over my face."[1] The images now follow one another rapidly. She moves quickly from the flood waters to speak of this same time as being when the arrows of her quiver were drunk with blood, and her presses fragrant with the best wine, and the "bridegroom with the ten wise virgins hath entered into my chambers and thereafter my belly hath swelled from the touch of my beloved and the bolt of my door hath been opened to my beloved, and after Herod being angry hath slain many children."[2] Though it seems as if this deluge of visions is a hodge-podge, in fact there is a meaningful theme connecting them and all that follows.

The flood is an image of the *solutio*, which is the process through which the earthly form of the original material is liquefied and destroyed. The *solutio*, like the *nigredo*, refers to the union of the original matter with a

power that destroys its initial form, thus opening the way for transformation. This repeats the theme from the previous chapter, but we move toward
symbolic expressions of fertility and birth. Yet these images are mixed with
those of death and destruction: first the arrows covered with blood, and
then Herod's slaughter of the children. The juxtaposition of death and
rebirth are announced in the title of this parable: "Of the Flood of Waters
and of Death, which the Woman both Brought in and Put to Flight." Sophia
is the divine force that both slays and leads to rebirth, and yet she herself is
the one undergoing the process of transformation. How are we to understand these images of destruction?

The biblical reference to arrows drunk with blood is from Deuteronomy
32:42, and von Franz points out that this reference equates Sophia with
God.[3] But the image of arrows is found in alchemy as well. In *The Chemical
Wedding of Christian Rosenkreutz*, Cupid punishes Christian for daring to
look at his sleeping mother, Venus, by cutting his hand with an arrow. This
seemingly minor event bares fruit later when Christian cannot go home at
the end of the story but must stay on at the castle for daring to behold Venus,
and Cupid's act was an expression of his great anger. The arrow here wounds
the adept so that he may never return to a normal life, having once gazed on
the beauty of the feminine, symbolized by Venus.[4] According to the commentator on *Hermes Unveiled*, the arrow refers to "the piercing quality of the
Secret Fire, which is stirred into action by a common, exterior, fire."[5]

The arrows that can slay are also related in this text to the forces of generation and renewal, just as they are in the *Aurora*. But let's go back to the
theme of the slaying of the children. The biblical reference is clear. Herod,
fearing the birth of the messiah, slays the innocent children to do away with
the threat. But what of this imagery in the alchemical context?

Nicholas Flammel, in his early and influential *Alchemical Hieroglyphics*,
wrote:

> On the last side of the fifth leaf (of the book of alchemy he had dis-
> covered) there was a *king* . . . who made to be killed in his presence
> by some *Soldiers* a great multitude of little *Infants* . . . the blood
> which Infants was afterwards by other Soldiers gathered up, and
> put in a great vessel, wherein the *Sun* and the *Moon* came to bathe
> themselves.[6]

Titus Burckhardt comments on this passage that the sacrificed children
refer to mercury:

This is none other than the "philosophic Quicksilver" which is the first manifestation of materia prima. Blood is the fundamental stuff of life. The holy innocents are like undefiled stirrings or out-breathings of the vital spirit which, before they can develop into ego conscious wills, are sacrificed by the king, in order to fill the vessel of the heart with their blood, so that sun and moon, spirit and soul, may bathe, be dissolved, and then united in it, and, hav-ing lost their old form, emerge from it rejuvenated.[7]

The creative use of the blood of the children, and their representing mer-cury or the undeveloped spirit, seems common in alchemical usage. In addition, there is the reference to the devouring of children by Saturn, which Thomas Vaughan likewise interprets as a fertilizing act when he writes that Saturn is the earth that swallows the rain and with it spiritual properties.[8]

The imagery of spring and new birth is closely related to the images of destruction in the *Aurora* because they refer to an internal process occurring within Sophia herself and, most likely, within her bridegroom as well. The children symbolize new beginnings, movements within the divine couple that must be killed in order for the energy that would have gone into them to be held back and used for transformation. While the children are killed, and the arrows filled with blood, the wines are pressed and the barns filled with corn. More importantly, the bridegroom and the ten wise virgins enter the bedchamber and impregnate Sophia. All other forms of expression, all other developments are sacrificed in order that the true child, the Philosopher's Stone, or *filius*, may be born. The *filius*, as we have seen, is the union of Sophia and the masculine aspect of the godhead. The slaughter of the children means that no growth can occur within either Sophia or God until their union is achieved. Not only does Sophia sacrifice her previous form, she gives up all independent and creative activity for the sake of the one truly creative act: union with God and the birth of the *filius*.

Psychoidal figures are autonomous and may live and act from their own wills for as long as they please. But once they are brought within the alchemist's laboratory and become the *prima materia*, their independence is at an end. The independent life of psychoidal figures is a fascinating topic. They seem to act according to their own unique nature, according to the powers that they incarnate. Sophia incarnates the forces of genera-tion, reproduction, and life as well as wisdom, but all of her natural activ-ities cease when alchemy begins. Yet, paradoxically, alchemy itself becomes nature, filling the barns and producing the pregnancy, but now the natural impulses of Sophia are directed to the one true goal. Just as human beings must give up their will in order to come into union with the divine, so the psychoidal figures must surrender their autonomy to come into their proper places. The spiritual power that would have gone into those autonomous directions are given over to the process itself. Sophia's arrows are filled with her own blood, as well as the blood of her partner, and, as Burckhardt said, this theme is related to the death of the original form. Form and independence are sacrificed for the greater union that creates the ally.

The individual experiencing psychoidal alchemy notices at this stage that Sophia ceases to manifest as an independent being, but is joined with her partner, and he or she can observe the transformations unfolding as this union takes place. One never experiences Sophia in quite the same way again, for she becomes part of the masculine divinity, as he becomes part of her. Each is half of the child born of their union.

This fact is disclosed as the text of *Aurora* moves to the discussion of the birth of the divine child:

> [A] light hath risen up in darkness . . . then the fullness of the time shall come when God shall send his Son . . . to whom he said of old time: Thou art my Son, today I have begotten thee. . . . That death which a woman brought into the world, this day hath a woman put to flight, and the barriers of hell are broken down; for death shall no more have dominion. . . .[9]

The *filius* is born and, with his birth, death is conquered, for the *filius* brings with his birth not only his own immortality but that of the alchemist as well. The union created between Sophia and God gives birth to the new *filius*, the whole Stone that shall live unbroken forever. With this act, the alchemist and the world itself are redeemed and Sophia-Mary, who gives birth to the divine child of redemption, rectifies death, which the sin of Eve had brought into the world.

In Gnosticism, Sophia was the cause of the fall and the one who helped redeem it. In the Bible, woman brought death into the world by her sin, and Mary brings Christ into the world to redeem it. In alchemy, Sophia is fallen nature that holds within itself the mysterious spirit whose liberation redeems not only her but life, itself. She brings death in her fall, she brings death to herself and to her spouse, she brings death to the innocent children, and thereby slays death itself. "It is meet therefore, my son, to make merry this day, for there shall be no more crying nor any sorrow, for the former things are passed away."[10]

Psychoidal alchemy is about the transformation of the forces that manifest in the psychoid realm as living entities. These living entities die to their own independence and become one with the ally. The split that existed between the masculine and feminine sides of God, as well as the chaos created by the independence of all the psychoidal forces, are indications of the fallen world. There is a tradition in the Kabbalah that when creation took place there was a breaking of the vessels designed to hold the divine light. When these vessels broke, the masculine and feminine parts of God turned away from each other and the divinity, as well as the world, ceased functioning as they were meant to. Healing consists of reuniting the two sides of God, and this is exactly the act of redemption portrayed in the *Aurora*. When Sophia and the masculine side of God are joined, the Stone is created, and with it the redemption of the universe achieved.

Sophia is the principle of life, the creatrix of life, and in her creative powers lies her wisdom. When this force and power are added to the ally, true immortality is achieved. With the birth of the Stone as a living entity that unites the feminine powers of creation with the masculine powers of will and ordering, a being that can never die is generated. As its partner, the human being shares in this immortality and "death shall no more have dominion."[11]

Sophia is thus transformed, as is the ally and the alchemist, but there is also the suggestion that there is a cosmic act of redemption that accompanies the birth of the *filius*. The text goes on to say that the "tenth groat, which was lost, is found, and the hundredth sheep is restored in the wilderness, and the number of our brethren from the fall of the angels is fully made up."[12] The act of redemption is depicted in the restoration of the number of angels from the fall, which is to say that the sin of Adam is redeemed, as is perhaps that of Lucifer. It is remarkable that a Christian may find in the completion of the work of alchemy a more comprehensive redemption than that offered in the traditional Church teachings.

How might we understand this act of cosmic redemption achieved through the union of Sophia and the masculine? Of course, from the larger perspective, this union brings together two aspects of the divinity and creates a new balance and harmony in God itself. To understand this, we must recall that the ally is that part of God that has manifested in the psychoid in order to make itself known to a human partner and to individuate; that is, to grow into its own unique wholeness. In order to do so, it must unite not only with its human partner, but also with other aspects of the divine nature, the most important of which is Sophia. By uniting with Sophia, the ally brings into itself not only the feminine divine principle, but also the wisdom that guides all of life. Moreover, it unites with the divine spirit that has been latent in all of nature and so unites with the psychoidal core of life itself.

The final parable of the *Aurora* explores this union in greater detail. The union of wife and husband, father and son, depicted in this parable points to a change in the divinity as it manifests in the psychoid, a transformation of the alchemist, and a redemption of cosmic proportions.

TRANSFORMATION OF THE SOUL

As in the previous parable, Thomas now speaks of the alchemical process associated with the changes so far described, but this time instead of speaking of the body he speaks of the soul:

> Take away his soul and give him back his soul, for the corruption
> of one is the generation of another, that is: Take from him the cor-
> rupting humour and add to him the connatural humour, through
> which shall come to pass his perfecting and life.[13]

In other words, the alchemist removes the soul, causing corruption or death, and then restores that soul, creating generation. That which is a corrupting influence is transformed into a connatural, or harmonious one, causing "his" perfection and life. The use of the male pronouns in the statement confuse the issue somewhat, but probably refer to the transformation occurring within the masculine side of the union, though we may easily suppose the same changes are happening within Sophia.

In chapter 3, I spoke of the psychoidal body as being the form in which spirit incarnated, and indicated that the body had to undergo transformation by uniting with the form of its psychoidal partner. The autonomous form died and was replaced by the *rebis*, the shared body in which both Sophia and the masculine god dwell as the new being—the ally. I also mentioned that the Stone consisted of body, soul, and spirit, and that all three were involved in the processes of alchemical transformation. Now it is the turn of the soul, which is separated from the body and purified in order to rejoin the body, which also has been purified.

Since the new, glorified body is that of the Stone, or of the ally, the soul of Sophia must be rejoined to the new body. In order to comprehend this fully, we must understand the alchemical notion of soul and its relationship with body and spirit. The interaction of these three components of the ally is amazingly complex, and once again I find it necessary to simplify. Let me first remind you of the context for this discussion. Thomas has presented the union of Sophia and the masculine and the consequent transformations. Not only does the emanated God transform, but the alchemist also finds immortality and the cosmos, itself, finds redemption. This is a reference to the final state, and the alchemical process of extracting and returning the soul is the means of achieving this state. It is clear that Thomas moves easily between the final state and the earlier stages of the process. The extraction of the soul and its consequent introduction to the body is not always the last stage, but in the present context I shall view it as one image of attaining the Stone. It is as if Thomas is saying: to find redemption, take away the soul and then return it, purified, to the new body previously created.

As Titus Burckhardt points out, alchemy "looks on the play of the powers of the soul from a purely cosmological point of view, and treats the soul as a 'substance' which has to be purified, dissolved, and crystallized anew."[14] He is referring to the human soul, but his statement is true of alchemy at every level. Metals have souls, humans have souls, and psychoidal entities have souls. In every case, these souls are treated as substances and subjected to various processes and transformations. Though different from the body, the soul, too, is a substance of sorts. And in this fact lies an important mystery of alchemy; soul, spirit, and body are not as different as we might imagine. All are substances, and this fact means that they can be "touched" and worked with. Though the soul is often viewed as intangible and invisible—as is spirit—in the psychoid, everything has substance. Thus the differences between body and soul are mitigated; body is form and soul inhabits that form. But the soul is substantial enough that, when removed from the body, it may be acted upon and purified. Recall that in chapter 1 I spoke of the dual process of a spiritual being entering the psychoid. The first step was for the being to put on a type of vibratory energy and the second, an image. The image is the body of the entity, and the vibratory energy it has assumed is its soul. Thus, when removed from the image, the psychoidal entity does not disappear, but remains as a "felt" energy and presence, with which the alchemist may work. But the alchemists have a lot more to say about soul.

George Ripley speaks of the soul as that which gives life to all things when he wrote that:

A soul it is, being betwixt heaven and earth,
Arising from the earth as air with water pure,
And causing life in every lively thing.[15]

The soul gives life to the body which gives the soul form. In *The Chemical Wedding of Christian Rosenkreutz*, when the bodies of the murdered king and queen are restored and in fact transmuted into bodies of numinous beauty, they remain lifeless and inert until their souls are inserted by means of a magical trumpet.[16] In *The Chemical Wedding*, the soul not only gives life; it is also an individual life, the life of the particular king and queen.

In its capacity to give life, the soul is equated with what in alchemy is called the "ferment." Edward Kelly quotes an alchemical text as saying that, "In our Stone the ferment is like the soul, which gives life to the dead body through the mediation of the spirit, or Mercury."[17] "This ferment is the soul. . . ." says the *Glory of the World*.[18] The soul as ferment is that which causes transformation in the body, for when the soul is extracted and then rejoined to the body, it alters the body to suit the soul's more perfect nature. Peter Bonus wrote:

> It is the body which retains the soul, and the soul can shew its power only when it is united to the body. Therefore when the artist sees the white soul arise, he should join it to its body in the same instant, for no soul can be retained without its body. This union takes place through the mediation of the spirit, for the soul cannot abide in the body except through the spirit, which gives permanence to their union, and this conjunction is the end of the work.[19]

There is a soul for each body, and the soul is of course extracted from the body, which leaves the body dead while the soul is being purified and transformed. Each metal, each body has its own proper soul which must be extracted and then reintroduced to the body. The author of the *Glory of the World* actually compares this process with the death and resurrection of Christ, through which his body and soul are made perfect and one.

PSYCHOIDAL TRANSFORMATION

The process should now be clear. The soul is extracted from the body and one way or another both are transformed. The soul needs the body or it will remain imperfect, and the body needs the soul or it will remain lifeless. The two together, after separation and conjunction, become perfect and likened to the glorified existence of the risen Christ. This transformation has profound implication for the human being who can undergo such an experience. But what of the psychoid figure that experiences this process?

When the souls of Sophia and of her partner are removed from their previous forms, two events occur. Their bodies are united to create the *rebis*, or the body of the ally, and their souls are then reintroduced into that body. Both bodies and souls are united and it is this union that gives rise to the new being, the ally. Alchemy is always about mixing and separating to create a new form. In this case, the new form is the union of masculine and feminine which produces a third entity that includes the original two, but is more than them. The soul of Sophia, or her essential nature, was removed from the form it had previously occupied. Once without form, it returned to the world of vibratory energy. During the time it remained in that place she received the influx of spiritual energies and powers, both strengthening and empowering her soul. But the true transformation of body and soul only occurs when the two are rejoined. The soul of Sophia enters her new body, that of the ally, and becomes the *rebis*. Two souls are now in one body.

The Nature of the Psychoidal Alchemy Experience

Psychoidal alchemy is not simply a theory but an experience. The soul of all psychoidal beings, as a type of subtle spirit-matter, is experienced as a vibration or moving energy. This is a felt experience; that is, it is not only seen with the eyes but has a definite qualitative sense related to it. Sophia, when she first appears, is in the form of a feminine being; yet to the eyes and feeling of the alchemist her body is not just this form, it consists of a vibratory energy. The form or image of Sophia is the body that contains the vibratory energy. The vibratory energy is of two kinds: it is universal and exists in a chaotic and unformed state, in which case it is known as spirit, or it has a unique quality to it that feels like Sophia or some other psychoidal being. When a spirit, unknowable in itself, enters the psychoid, its essence forms the subtle energy to express itself, and this is the soul of the entity. When it takes the next step and assumes a form or image, this is its body.

I have stressed and repeated this difficult concept because it is important to realize that the soul and the body are both substances that can be seen and felt. When the soul is removed from the body, the previously living Name looses its form and in this sense "dies," but its soul remains as vibratory energy of a unique kind. In meditative and visionary states the alchemist works with the vibratory energy that is Sophia. Through this work, the alchemist becomes more conscious of her, and she becomes more conscious of herself. She undergoes a process of purification, and when the time comes for her to enter a new image, it is no longer that of her self as she was, but that of the ally. This new image is created spontaneously from the union of Sophia's soul with that of her masculine partner, which the alchemist beholds as well. Most of the time the alchemist is a witness only, for there is nothing to do but see these subtle forms and their interaction. When they join together they create a new image that will hold them, and that image is the body for a very powerful psychoidal being, the ally.

The soul is the conscious essence and being of the individual. The soul of Sophia is her own essential nature, the very core of her nature and individuality. This, too, is a felt experience, which betrays any attempt to convey it in words. Her essence, however, may be said to be something like the dancing sparkle of life—she is the principle of life itself. She is a joyful, creative manifestation of all possible expressions of living forms, and she is the knowledge of them all. As the very principle of life, she is the center of all souls and all souls belong to her. Her felt sense is one of the deepest joys imaginable, the joy of life in its youth, of creativity in its ecstatic flow of creation. All good things come with and from her. But when first incarnated in the vibrational energy her powers are still limited and darkened. As with all psychoidal beings, her incarnation in the psychoid takes place in an imperfect body. So she must be removed from it, and finally placed in an image that allows her essence to shine forth as part of the Stone.

The image that holds Sophia and her divine partner is not like the previous image in which they both manifested before their union. The new image alters and becomes pure light. The new image is a union of an imaginal form and light. The imaginal form takes on greater numinosity, and the light is the vibratory energy raised to a higher level. Both soul and body are thus transmuted into light. The vibratory energy becomes light, and the image that holds this light shines with it and is luminous. The body and soul of the *filius* is a glorified light, not like physical light, but a luminosity that is a body of perfection.

The *filius* is light which is the center of all things, and whoever beholds it has come to the place of the hidden wonders of God and may experience new miracles every day. Through this light, which is the soul-body of the Stone, the beholder, according to Thomas Vaughan, may "know their Region of Light and . . . enter into the treasures thereof, for then thou mayst converse with spirits and understand the nature of invisible things."[20] And as Jung writes, the Stone is "a light above all lights."[21]

The vibratory energy of the psychoid soul becomes, as the Stone, a pure and celestial light that, like physical light, is neither one thing nor the other, neither body nor spirit, but both and neither. As the body of Sophia undergoes transformation before the eyes of the alchemist, and unites with the purified body, it becomes one with this pure light and as this contemplated light, opens the alchemist's vision to things divine, he or she now beholds the incarnation of Sophia's soul in the light body of the ally, which is now her body, too. The vision of the alchemist also beholds that where there was one, there are now two, though one in light, two in individuality and presence. That is, the souls of both God and Sophia are preserved in the ally, which in itself, is the union of soul and body as light.

The conversion of body and soul to light is the most profound experience I have ever witnessed. The incarnation of Sophia is therefore not in the human psyche, but in the body of the ally. The human psyche could not contain such light—it can witness it and can unite with it through the love of the ally, but it cannot hold it.

When this union occurs, Sophia is purified and her powers, joined to the ally, become clearer and more pronounced. She is not diminished by such union, but fulfilled by it, as is the ally whose ultimate task it is to incarnate the divine powers. As for the alchemist who not only witnesses this conjunction, but continues to live in relationship with it, the light continues to produce its miracles day by day and to reveal the hidden secrets of the divinity, for Wisdom is made manifest and united to the power and center of the ally. And, therefore, as Thomas has written: "There shall be no more crying nor any sorrow, for the former things are passed away."

CHAPTER 7

THE GATES OF BRASS:
FROM CHAOS TO ORDER

In the first two parables, the *Aurora* has spoken of body and soul and we might expect it to proceed to spirit as the third ingredient of the *prima materia* and the Stone. However, there is a repetition that occurs in the third parable, a redoing, as it were, of the last section. Once more the biblical quotations make it clear that Sophia is speaking as a divinity. She is once more in prison and is hungry, seeking a place to rest and yearning for the gifts of the Holy Spirit. She says that, "there is no soundness in me," and seeks the cleansing grace of pure water. Once more, she speaks of the time of liberation when she will have the power of penetration and liquefaction and will "be glorified by God."[1] She refers to the rivers of Babylon, and the Babylonian Captivity when the Jews were held in bondage. There is so much in this section that we cannot discuss every image. I once again refer the interested reader to von Franz's commentary, which gives the more traditional Jungian perspective as well as theological amplifications. For our purposes, I shall focus on the major themes that we have already seen and take note of additional amplifications made in this section. Thomas presumably had a reason to go back once more to the state of captivity that the *anima mundi* finds herself in, but perhaps adds some new information, as well.

I suspect he returned to the original state because the liberation of the psychoidal figure from her state of semi-consciousness and the consequent redemption of the world is certainly no easy task. It is a work of a lifetime for some, and an endeavor requiring a supreme effort. In all the sections until the last, the movement from imprisonment to freedom is almost too quick, as if Thomas saw in his ecstasy the possibility for which he and Sophia both yearned, but were not yet able to achieve. There is another meaning for this repetition. In my experience, processes by which a psychoidal figure unites with the center are not accomplished all at once. They proceed more slowly in increments, a gradual union developing as the essence or soul of the psychoidal entity is gradually added to the *rebis*. Each time this occurs there is ecstasy and the thrilling delight of freedom and transformation, but this does not mean that the process is complete. It must be repeated over and over again until the alchemist achieves the final union.

In the meditative states through which psychoidal alchemy unfolds, the alchemists perceive the admixture of the soul and body in gradual stages. Recall that from the alchemical and the psychoidal point of view, the soul is a substance that the alchemists feel and "touch" as it is added to its body. But if too much were added at once there is a great chance of spoiling the whole process by overwhelming the alchemist's consciousness. Even though I have called the alchemist a witness, it should not be forgotten that he or she witnesses not simply with his or her eyes but with his or her felt sense, which includes the alchemist's whole consciousness. Too much "witnessing" can be harmful. So the work of redemption unfolds incrementally and the return to the unredeemed state is necessary.

Sophia cries out in pain in this state and the alchemist who works with her feels this pain with equal sharpness. The golden light regresses and becomes once more the vibratory energy, and the experience of this energy is painful when compared with the light. We must not give in to despair at this repetition, though the physical and psychological pain caused by it is great, but remember that each time the process is repeated the golden light is more powerful, more beautiful, and more stable.

There are several motifs worth noting as Thomas returns to embrace the fallen Sophia and once more work on her redemption. The number seven is repeated three times: in reference to the gift of the Holy Spirit, seven woman seeking one man, and the Jews' seventy years in captivity. Seventy numerologically is the same as seven. Von Franz interprets the seven as referring to the seven planetary spirits trapped in the Earth, and as the seven metals corresponding to them.[2] This is no doubt correct, and refers to the process whereby Sophia gathers the powers of the celestial world to herself to aid in her redemption, while redeeming those powers lost in the world.

TRANSFORMATION OF THE SOUL

Once the alchemists have witnessed the extracting of the soul from Sophia's body, the soul ascends to the higher world. While the body is purified, the soul, too, experiences transformation. The body has undergone a transformation into the body of the ally, a body, which, when revivified, is a body of light. The soul, though it retains its individuality, must transform before it is able to join the ally in the new, glorified body. The ascension of the soul has two effects. It is liberation of the soul from the old body, which is the prison it found itself in, and an expansion of its own natural abilities and potentialities. How is the soul prepared for its transformation, a transformation that not only multiplies its own powers and essence but also contains the powers of the *filius*?

In the *Aurora*, there is one clear process that presents itself. This concerns the seven daughters of Sion who undergo changes as the parable unfolds. Thomas first calls them haughty and says that "they walked with stretched-out necks and winkings of their eyes and made a noise and went at a measured pace." [3] In other words, the planetary spirits, emblematic of the psychoidal forces, were arrogant and not oriented toward the center. They expressed only their own nature and there was no harmony. In their transformation lies the hint concerning the soul's transformation while separated from the body. As von Franz indicated, the seven daughters are the seven planetary powers related to the seven metals. The celestial powers of the planets are essential in alchemy. In some cases the alchemists argue that the influx of planetary emanations influenced which metal would form in what location; a large dose of Venus, for example, would produce copper. But there is a deeper meaning of the celestial influences in alchemy; one derived from Gnostic and Kabbalistic sources.

Jung wrote that Gerald Dorn, a noted alchemist and disciple of Paracelsus, divided the work into three stages of union. The second one occurred when the body and the soul were rejoined, the same stage that the third parable of the *Aurora* presents. At this juncture in the alchemical undertaking, Dorn "drew the 'influence' of the planets . . . into his quintessence . . ."[4] Of course, this was not simply a physical procedure, but as Jung says, the alchemists felt it "as a magically effective action which, like the substance itself, imparted magical qualities."[5] The work with the planets added their magical powers to the Stone itself, or, in this case, to the psychoidal entity becoming one with Stone.

Many other alchemists speak of this process as well. They saw the planets not as physical objects, but as spiritual entities, each with certain characteristics. Their influence on life was immense, and if their power could be channeled into a medium or substance under the control of the alchemist, that power would serve the process of making the Stone. Paracelsus says, for example, that "none can deny that the superior stars and influences of heaven have very great weight in transient and mortal affairs" and he also says that, "It is possible to man himself to bring these into a certain medium, wherein they may effectually operate, whether this medium be a metal, a stone, or an image."[6]

The planets are clearly spiritual agents of some kind. Within the psyche they would correspond to the archetypes, but in the psychoid they would be centers of spiritual power manifesting as psychoidal figures. Each would have its own particular characteristic and power, but whatever power they possess, the alchemist must find a way to concentrate that power within their substance. They accomplished this by uniting the separated soul with these spiritual forces that then remained with the soul as it incarnated in the body. The Emerald Tablet, considered by many to be the summary of the Great Work, states:

> With great capacity it ascends from earth to heaven. Again it descends to earth, and takes back the power of the above and the below.
>
> Thus you will receive the glory of the distinctiveness of the world. All obscurity will flee from you.
>
> This is the whole most strong strength of all strength, for it overcomes all subtle things, and penetrates all solid things.[7]

The soul, separated from its body, rises to the upper realm and encounters the spirits that abide therein. It puts on their power and descends with them once more into the new body prepared for it. Notice that the power gained, according to The Emerald Tablet, is the ability to penetrate all solid things. This is the very power mentioned in the Aurora as belonging to Sophia on the day of resurrection.

We are now in a position to understand the seven daughters. At first they were haughty and independent. The psychoidal powers are not related to Sophia originally, which is part of the reason she remains imprisoned. They do as they wish and create what they wish, so that the psychoidal world is chaotic, and its influences on our world are neither considered nor ordered, but inharmonious and chaotic. But the work of alchemy humbles them and orients them to one center:

> In that day when seven women took hold of one man, saying: We eat our own bread and wear our own apparel, why dost thou not defend our blood, which is poured out as water round about Jerusalem?[8]

To reiterate, the seven women are the seven planetary powers, which now take hold of one man. The one man is the ally, which acts as the center around which the psychoidal powers are now organized. Though these forces are still independent and alive in their own right, for they have their own bread and wear their own apparel, they are centered around the one man and around Jerusalem, the sacred city which serves as a symbol of the center. God answers their complaint in the next line by saying they should be at rest, until the time when all is saved and the Lord "shall have washed away the filth of his daughters of Sion with the spirit of wisdom and understanding; then will ten acres of vineyard yield one little measure and thirty bushels of seed yield three bushels."[9] The daughters of Sion, the psychoidal powers, will be washed with the spirit of wisdom, (of Sophia) and then will participate in the general redemption. When Sophia takes these psychoidal powers in hand she will guide them with wisdom, knowing what is right and where power should flow in the true order of things. They will no longer be fully independent, but will serve Sophia and her spouse in the creation of the *filius*.

Each planet in alchemy had its own type of power and influence, and the alchemists were much indebted to astrology for their conceptions of these powers. The psychoid is filled with powers, likened, as I have said, to Names of God or even Kaballistic Sephiroth. But in the alchemical worldview, these powers, which should serve God and should work together as a whole, are polluted and corrupted. They are haughty and are like archons in the Gnostic myths that obey no higher authority, but do as they will. Sophia, as wisdom, should guide not only our life in the world, but should also order the workings of these archons. This she cannot do until her own reformation, which occurs with the separation and return of her soul.

Viewed impersonally, there are forces in the universe that operate without restraint, and the chaos that ensues is the source of evil and discord in our world and in all the worlds. Recall my dream of the cosmic mandala in which all things had a certain place and not being in their proper place caused evil. I spoke of it earlier as relating to the individual's ignorance of Sophia, but it is now apparent that there is a larger view that we must take. The psychoidal spirits must also be in their proper place, and unless they are, evil continues unrestrained. Sophia is the personification of the wisdom that knows the place of all things and can lead them to their proper places, effecting a general redemption of the universe. It is through Sophia that we can learn who and what we are and it is through her that the planetary powers can learn who they are and what they serve. But only when Sophia, as feminine wisdom, is united with the masculine power of God does this become possible. Through the union of wisdom and power, unity prevails.

The image of unity is apparent in the statement that when the daughters of Sion are washed with the spirit of wisdom, "then will ten acres of vineyard yield one little measure and thirty bushels of seed yield three bushels. He that understandeth this shall not be moved forever."[10] Von Franz comments that, "The reduction from thirty to three is a *reduction of the plurality to the essential*: the chaotic contents of the unconscious are reduced to their essential expression."[11] As I have explained, the same is true on the psychoidal level. The diverse powers are reduced to a single power; the central point created by the union of Sophia and her lover with the resultant manifestation of the ally. When we understand this, we are "not moved forever" for we shall have reached the essential mystery of the unity of all things in the marriage of wisdom and power. Not being moved forever results from the central point, for when it emerges, it remains forever. It is an eternal partner to whom we may cling without interference.

I have been speaking of this process in its impersonal and cosmic aspect. For the psychoidal alchemist, the work certainly has this cosmic dimension to it, but it has a personal one as well. The alchemist relates to Sophia through love, and communes with the ally through love. Through the love the alchemist feels for Sophia, not as a cosmic principle of wisdom, but as a living being and the quintessence of the feminine, he or she marries her as much as the masculine God does. The alchemist is the central focal point through which Sophia and God unite, for it is in the alchemist's witnessing alone that this union comes into being. He or she at the same time greets the birth of the ally with deepest joy. Love is the glue that binds the two cosmic principles, viewed as individual and beloved figures, in a union that promises to create order in the psychoidal realm, and thereby in the human realm, as well. We cannot hope that only a few having these experience will overcome the forces of division and competition between the archons, but if a few hundred had such an experience, or even a few thousand, who could say what the effect on the world might be?

CHAPTER 8

OF THE PHILOSOPHIC FAITH: THE NATURE OF SPIRIT

The *Aurora's* fourth "Parable of the Philosophic Faith" is a very cumbersome one, in which the author first presents Sophia speaking once more, then moves into a theological discussion of the Trinity, and finally presents an alchemical characterization of the powers and influence of the Holy Spirit. In the previous parables, Thomas had presented the body and the soul, two thirds of the great alchemical trinity, and we can expect he would eventually present the nature of spirit. This parable is in fact a very detailed presentation of the role of spirit in the alchemical work. For the sake of simplicity and in order to stay on target, I shall only discuss the sections of this parable that deal with the spirit; these form the last part of the parable.

THE NATURE OF SPIRIT

Thomas returns to his favorite number seven in order to elucidate all of the attributes of the spirit. He argues that there are seven attributes, the first of which is fire. The Holy Spirit or the alchemical spirit is like fire and it warms the earth which is cold, dead, and dry. Thomas quotes several alchemical writers to amplify his point, including the author of the *Book of the Quintessence,* to the effect that fire penetrates, subtilizes, and consumes all material, earthly parts. He also quotes Calet as saying that the spirit warms the cold, and Senior who instructs the alchemist to set the male upon the female, the warm upon the cold.[1]

The symbol of fire is associated with Sophia and with the boundless fire of the universal spirit, which gave life to all things. The Holy Spirit is the universal spirit that is related to and personified by Sophia, sparking all of life and giving motion and vitality to all things. Whereas the soul is individual, the spirit is universal. It is the activity of God as it manifests in all things.

However, Thomas only addresses its effect on the body in this parable: it warms and consumes the body. Again referring to the *Book of the Quintessence*, Thomas writes that, "as long as fire hath matter, it ceaseth not to act, seeking to imprint its form on the passive substance."[2] The spirit acts on the body in such a way as to consume it, so long as there is anything to consume. The role of the spirit is to ignite the impure body and purify it, destroying its previous form and allowing another one to manifest. Yet, if the power of the fire were unchecked, it would continuously destroy all form but its own. In other words, the spirit is originally antithetical to the body; the impersonal destroying the personal, not just in its original form, but utterly. This would obviously be a disaster to the individual being who would be completely consumed by the impersonal spirit, and this often happens to those who do not know how to protect themselves from the burning and absorbing power of the spirit. Many spiritual traditions of course seek just this consumption of the earth by the fire, of the body by the spirit, of the personal by the impersonal, but such is not the way of alchemy. Nor is it the natural way of the spirit itself, as Thomas shows us by explaining the second property of spirit:

> In the second place he extinguisheth the intense imprinted fire by ignition, of which saith the Prophet: A fire was kindled in their congregation, and a flame burned the wicked upon earth; he extinguisheth this fire by its own temperament, whence it is added: Thou art coolness in the heat.[3]

He also refers to Avicenna as saying that in a "thing in which there is burning, the first thing that is released from it is a fiery virtue, which is milder and more worthy than the virtues of the other elements."[4] The fire that is spirit is also a coolness in the heat, and by its action it releases another fiery virtue, which is, however, mild and more worthy than the other elements, a reference to the fifth element of which the Stone is composed. Though hell-fire is still related to the fire of the spirit (for it burns the wicked), the fire does not constantly and eternally consume the earth, thereby destroying all form. Rather, it releases a fire within the form, and then itself extinguishes the second fire. The spirit becomes cool when the inner fire of the earth or form is released. This inner fire is the secret fire hidden within matter.

We must round off our threefold description of body, soul, and spirit with a paradox. The spirit is that which encloses the body which itself encloses the soul, but also contains within itself the spirit. The divine spirit is within all matter and yet outside of all matter. In terms of the psychoid, each psychoidal being contains within itself a spark of the divine spirit, just as each human being does. Yet this spirit lies dormant until heated up by the universal spirit, which triggers it into fire. The latter fire creates a process destroying the form and so enabling a transformation to occur. Lest the fire continue out of control, the external spiritual power turns into its opposite and puts the interior fire out. This is a fascinating commentary on the action of the spirit which remains destructive and fiery until the inner fire is triggered and the old form destroyed, at which point all is turned cool, and what remains is a new virtue or essence of the body; a new element that will create a new type of body or of form.

The spirit will act in a destructive and consuming fashion until something within the form being acted upon begins the process of transformation, which is then regulated and controlled by the spirit itself. The goal of psychoidal alchemy is to bring the forces of the psychoid into harmony with the center of the psychoid, or the ally. The divine spirit aims spontaneously toward this goal, and will be the fires of hell until the psychoidal entity begins transformation, when the spirit turns mild. Applied to a human being, this would mean that the divine spirit is hell to him or her unless he or she releases his or her own inner fire and accepts death and rebirth. What looks like evil can be turned to good once transformation begins. If a person refuses to allow the inner fires of transformation to emerge, he or she would remain in the outer hellfire. The burning action of fire, which would be experienced as pain or even evil, can only be transformed when the inner spirit, united to the true form of a person, the Self, emerges. This emergence requires a willingness to give up all false identities and become the Self.

There is another mystery contained in this imagery. Thomas said earlier that fire imposes form, seeking to imprint its form on the passive substance. As indicated, if spirit imposes its own form on the person or psychoidal being exposed to it, the impersonal would dissolve the personal. Since this process is not allowed to continue forever, this is a temporary phase of the whole work. During this phase, the body is destroyed and becomes imprinted with the form of the spirit; the body becomes spirit. Yet once the body is purified and takes on the form of the spirit, it may be said that the body has become spirit, but simultaneously the spirit has become body. In other words, the form or the new body prepared for the soul of the psychoidal being is spirit itself, the divine spirit which is at the same time the body of the ally. The next property of the spirit demonstrates this paradox completely.

Just as the spirit is fire and coolness, so, too, is it water, which "liquefieth the hardness of the earth and dissolveth its condensed and exceedingly compact parts."[5] The rain of the spirit melts the body, but now the body reacts upon the spirit: "The spirit dissolveth the body (and softeneth it) and the body hardeneth the spirit."[6] There is an exchange here, for as the spirit dissolved the hardness of the earth, the earth hardens the spirit, preparing the way for the spirit itself to become body. The spirit is fire and water. As fire it destroys the body, and as water it purifies the body, once more dissolving the form that previously existed, but now spirit is caught by the body as well and begins to lose its incorporeal and fiery nature to become something of the earth and body. The spirit that has destroyed the form of the body has itself lost its own form. This leads to the next stage in the work, which Thomas likens to the next and fourth attribute of the spirit: enlightenment.

The divine spirit brings light, purging the darkness of the mind and leading night into day.[7] This is the process known as the *albedo*, when the blackness of the *nigredo* turns white, and the stage of death moves toward rebirth. I have mentioned that the body of the ally may be said to be that of light, and now the body takes on the attributes of light as it unites with the spirit. At this stage of the work, according to the *Book of the Quintessence*: "Thou seest a wondrous light in the darkness."[8] Thomas also quotes the alchemist Morienus to sum up this transition to the *albedo*: "Already we have taken away the black and have made the white, with the salt [and] [a] natron, that is with the spirit."[9] But the union of the body and spirit is not yet complete, for as we move to the fifth aspect of spirit, this union finally is achieved.

According to Thomas, the fifth aspect of the spirit is that it separates the pure from the impure, separating moreover that which is unlike and uniting that which is alike. This capacity and power of the spirit sets in motion a process known as circulation which Alphidius, quoted by Thomas, sums up as follows: "Earth is liquefied and turned into water, water is liquefied and turned into air, air is liquefied and turned into fire, and fire is liquefied and turned into glorified earth."[10] Through the operations of the spirit, all impurities are expelled from the body, which loses its form in the process. But as the spirit continues to act on the body, and the body exerts its influence on the spirit, the circulation occurs, and beginning with impure body we end with the pure and glorified body. The glorified body is the body as spirit and the spirit as body. The glorification of new form that has emerged means it is divine and immortal.

The Circulatio

Before going on to the next attribute of the spirit, which finally brings soul into the process, it is necessary to discuss how other alchemists viewed the *circulatio* and the union of body and spirit.

The spirit interacts with the body of the psychoid entity in such a way as to destroy it, then checks the process of destruction by cooling off. It acts then as liquid, or the divine water, which loosens the body and hardens the spirit. This triggers the circulation that begins with earth and ends with earth, but at a higher level of existence. The form that previously existed is gone, replaced by the form that the divine spirit creates, thereby becoming the form of divinity itself. The form of divinity is the *filius*, or the ally, which is the highest form of the psychoid. Spirit is the impersonal manifestation of the godhead, which is experienced in the psychoid as the vibratory energy. When the image or body of a psychoid being is united with the spirit, the spirit becomes body and the body becomes spirit: a union of opposites that creates the form of the Stone, or the body of light.

Other alchemists describe this process of spirit becoming body as well. George Ripley summarizes the whole process best:

> If you therefore will exalt the bodies,
> First you augment them with the spirit of life,
> Till in time the earth be well subtilized,
> By natural rectifying of every Element,
> Exalting them up into the firmament,
> Then much more precious shall they be than gold,
> Because of the quintessence which they do hold.
>
> For when the cold has overcome the heat,
> Then into water the air shall be turned,
> And so two contraries together shall meet,
> Till either with the other right well agree,
> So into air the water as I tell thee,
> When heat of cold has got domination,
> Shall be converted by craft of our circulation.
>
> And of the air then fire you shall have,
> By loosening, putrefying and subliming,
> And fire you have of the earth material,
> Thus by craft dissevering your elements,
> Most especially well calcining your earth,

And when they be each one made pure,
Then do they hold all of the first nature.[11]

The process Ripley describes is exactly the circulation that Thomas speaks of. The first nature is the quintessence, and the body has by the end of this process reached its perfection. The perfect form has been achieved, in which the soul may find a perfect home. For some alchemical writers, the soul is that which joins the spirit and the body and allows their union to occur. In whatever way a particular alchemist views this process, at some point the soul must be added to the mix of spirit and body. Thomas therefore moves next to a discussion of soul.

The sixth attribute of the spirit is its ability to exalt the lowly, for by this means it "bringeth to the surface the soul deep and hidden in the bowels of the earth."[12] Thomas now cites another series of biblical and alchemical references to explain this function of the spirit. According to the philosophers, "Whosoever shall make the hidden manifest knoweth the whole work."[13] He quotes Alphidius once more to the effect that unless the soul is raised, nothing further can happen because "through it and with it and in it all the work is done."[14] There are texts that argue that the soul is that which enables spirit and body to unify, and Alphidius may be hinting at the same thing. This makes perfect sense if we remember that the body is form, and the spirit is imposing its form on the body to create a new form, but the body is an individual and personal form, while the spirit is impersonal. The soul, as the essence of individuality and the embodiment of that which makes something unique, serves to unite the impersonal spirit with the personal form in a new unity that is both personal and impersonal. Yet were the soul to be lost somehow, the quality of individuality would be lost as well, since the form of the individual was at first destroyed by the spirit. It can only come back into play through the agency of the soul.

Thomas next speaks of the glorification of the body with the seventh and last attribute of the spirit: it "inspireth." It breathes into the earthly body, making it spiritual. This summarizes the whole of the work discussed in the fourth parable. It finally can be said that the essential nature of spirit is to purify and glorify the body and to free it from "the corrupting humidity"[15] which is to make it immortal. The whole discussion of the spirit has concerned its union with the body and the preparation of the body for the new embodiment of the soul. The elevation of the soul, briefly mentioned in this chapter, is the only reference to the soul work in the whole section and, in fact, Thomas has little more to say of the soul in the remainder of the book. The soul work came earlier, when he discussed the death created by the separation of the body and the soul and the soul's putting on the planetary powers. The soul work was completed, and it only remained to transform body through the agency of spirit to finish the work. Of course, the new and glorified body has become the house in which the soul incarnates. Though Thomas does not explicitly mention the incarnation, the next parable opens with the declaration that Wisdom has built herself a house, not only for herself but for humans as well. We shall examine this house in some detail, but to conclude this chapter it is essential that you understand that the work of the spirit has been to transform the old body into the new house in which Sophia now abides. She, or her essence, her soul, has returned to the glorified body and thus created her new dwelling place. The new dwelling place is the body of light, the ally.

CHAPTER 9

THE HOUSE THAT WISDOM BUILT:
THE INCARNATION OF THE DIVINE

The fifth parable is unique in the *Aurora*, being devoted not only to the nature of the Stone but also to the experience of the alchemist who attains the Stone. It also deals with the characteristics that the alchemist needs to create the Stone, and even speaks of the relationship between the alchemist and the Stone. There is also some confusion between the alchemist and Wisdom, but this should not be surprising. The inner work of the alchemist parallels the psychoidal work, and, as I explained in the introduction, alchemy could occur at all levels at once. The Stone can be the alchemist's Self as well as the transformed psychoidal figure, depending on the level of the work in which the alchemist is engaged. Mostly, Thomas describes the nature of Wisdom herself, but in this parable he spends more time on the alchemist.

The opening lines of this parable are, "Wisdom hath built herself a house, which if any man enter in he shall be saved."[1] As I mentioned, the house that Wisdom built is her new body, the divine form given to her by spirit and created through the union of the impersonal spirit and the personal soul. Sophia now moves into that house, as her soul reincarnates in the transformed body. But Sophia is a psychoidal being. Her new form, which is also the body of the ally, has a tremendous impact on the human being. All those men and women who find her house are saved and share in its wonders. Psychoidal alchemy works with nonhuman forces and beings, but the transformation of such beings impacts human life. One who seeks Sophia before her transformation finds only a shadow of her being. But the alchemist who transforms Sophia through the processes so far described discovers a magical and wondrous being, fully endowed with her powers

and her capacity to guide and ensoul, for Wisdom has built herself a treasure house through the agency of alchemy.

Can others find this house created through the help of the alchemists,
or is it for the alchemist alone? Thomas implies that once the house has
been created, any who find it are blessed by it. The implication is that the
work of psychoidal alchemy creates a power and a being meant not only for
the alchemist, but also for any who seek Sophia. I have always felt that each
individual must do his or her own work, and that no one can do it for him
or her. I still believe that in large part, but it also seems to me now that anyone who does psychoidal alchemy impacts the journeys and experiences of
those who seek Sophia in whatever way they choose. Sophia does not belong
to the individual alone, she is a cosmic principle, and if that principle is
strengthened by alchemy, she becomes stronger for all beings and all life. To
what extent I cannot say, but it is enough to know that alchemical work is
never just for the individual doing it, but is for all beings.

Wisdom has built herself a house and a marvelous house it is. Thomas
once more enters a near ecstatic state as he tries to describe the new house
of Wisdom. In many ways, this parable is the most complex and descriptive
we have yet encountered in the *Aurora*. In the description of the house and
its thirteen properties are many of the secrets of the Stone. The parable contains a plethora of biblical and alchemical references, which, unlike the last
parable, all deserve consideration. I shall amplify most of these images, and
to avoid confusion you should bear in mind that in this parable Wisdom
once again speaks for herself and that almost every image is descriptive of
the house she has built. Wisdom not only portrays the attributes of the
house, but the alchemical rewards it offers as well as what is necessary to
achieve those rewards. Wisdom is very clearly equated with the divinity
again, so that she speaks as God or, alchemically, as the *filius*. With the creation of the house she has entered final stages of the work in which the
transformed Sophia achieves permanent life and stability. Though the
union with the masculine is not yet announced, Sophia in her own right is
close to being the Stone, and as such she presents herself in this parable.

Von Franz offers two amplifications for the image of the house in her
commentary. The first, not surprisingly, is from Senior who compares the
lapis (stone) and a house, and then, in a more developed fashion, Alphidius
amplifies the house symbol. She quotes Alphidius as follows:

> I will show thee the place of this stone. . . . Know, my son, that this
> knowledge is in a certain place and that this place is everywhere.

The place is the four elements, and they are four doors. . . . This is
the treasure-house in which are treasured up all the sublime things
of science or wisdom or the glorious things which cannot be pos-
sessed. . . [2]

Von Franz discusses this quotation in great detail and her commentary is
worth looking into. There are also other references to the house in alchemy.
Figure 10 shows the king in the house eating the apples of immortality. This
image from Michael Maier's *Atalanta Fugiens* derives from the *Turba
Philosophorum*, in which one finds the following:

Take that tree, and build a house about it, which shall wholly surround the same, which shall also be circular, dark, encircled by
dew, and shall have placed on it a man of a hundred years; shut and
secure the door lest dust or wind should reach them. Then in the
time of 180 days send them away to their homes. I say that man

*Figure 10. The alchemical house is the house that Sophia builds—her new
body. The alchemist experiencing this body attains immortality in union with
Sophia.*

shall not cease to eat of the fruit of that tree to the perfection of the number [of the days] until the old man shall become young. O what marvelous natures, which have transformed the soul of that old man into a juvenile body, and the father is made into the son! Blessed be thou, O most excellent God![3]

The house in the *Turba* is the place of mysterious transformation and rejuvenation, and one that holds the promise of immortality. So, too, is the house of Wisdom. Anyone who finds the house is blessed beyond measure for "great is the multitude of thy sweetness which thou has hidden for them that enter this house; which eye hath not seen nor ear heard, neither hath it entered into the heart of man."[4] This biblical reference to Psalm 30 serves to equate Wisdom with God, and her house is therefore a heavenly abode wherein one finds ecstasy, delight and immortality.

Perhaps the earliest reference to the house is that found in the writings of the early alchemist Zosimos, who flourished around the fourth century A.D. He wrote of building a temple from a "single stone, like to white lead, to alabaster, to Proconnesian marble, with neither end nor beginning in its construction."[5]

The house is often a symbol of the center and thus of the Self. Clearly it is the Stone, or the place of the Stone as it incarnates in form. Sophia's house is her new form, created from the work in the previous parables. She has come alive in a whole new way, restored and rejuvenated herself, and therefore holds the gifts of immortality and healing for others. Thomas wrote, "Whosoever by his science shall open this house shall find therein an unfailing living fount that maketh young, wherein whoever is baptized, [he] shall be saved and can no more grow old."[6] This section of the parable is about the alchemist who is able to find his or her way into Sophia's house, and reaps the rewards thereof. Clearly that reward is spiritual awakening and eternal life, understood not in a physical sense but in the psychoidal one. Those who find the way to union with Sophia experience her wisdom, guidance, and her eternally renewing energies of life. She is the awakened and transformed life-generating fountain and both men and women who drink of her waters "shall neither hunger nor thirst anymore."[7] Sophia is the principle of enlightenment, and the alchemist who has helped her find a new body experiences that enlightenment. From the perspective of psychoidal alchemy, enlightenment is a union with Sophia and the ally as psychoidal figures, and such a union feeds the human partner in every conceivable way and constantly renews them with spiritual vigor. Union with Sophia means a loving relationship with the source of life's energies. These images do not mean that we never become ill or die to the physical body but that, while in the body, life is a never-ceasing source of riches, for even the hard times are gold when shared with Sophia. The alchemist truly enters the house of Sophia, which means that, in union with her, we share in her new form, in her psychoidal body, forever. Just as the ally and Sophia share one form, so, too, does the alchemist share this form and live therein with her two lovers.

In what von Franz informs us is a corrupted text,[8] Thomas speaks of children and their elders finding a way to open the house and when they do "face to face and eye to eye they shall look upon all the brightness of the sun and moon."[9] The text concerning the children and the elders is difficult to understand, though there may be some references to the famous idea of alchemy being children's play and of having to become as a little child to gain the kingdom of heaven. In any case, if one enters one beholds the brightness of the sun and the moon. This is a reference to the union of the sun and moon which symbolizes the *coniunctio*, or the union wherein all the opposites join together to form a new totality. Here is the first reference to the fact that the house is not only that of Sophia but belongs to God as well, who, we may suppose, has undergone parallel processes with Sophia in order to prepare for His own incarnation in the new form of the *filius*. The brightness of the sun and the moon is also a reference to the light, which characterizes the form of the *filius*.

The brightness generated by the sun and the moon is the light generated by the union of the opposites. Von Franz believes that this brightness is some sort of supernatural light and she is no doubt correct.[10] I wrote earlier that the body of the ally is light, and therefore within the form of Sophia, we would also experience this same light. It is generated from the union of the sun and moon, or the masculine and feminine, which here denotes Sophia and her partner. The alchemist who finds his or her way beholds the light generated by God and Sophia and thereby experiences enlightenment.

THE ENLIGHTENMENT OF THE ALCHEMIST

I have mentioned some of these experiences before, but now seems a good place to list them all, or as many as I may. Keeping in mind that it is the union of the masculine and Sophia and the emergence of the ally that creates these experiences, you will perceive that the alchemist is a benefactor of the cosmic shift that has occurred through their union. The psychoidal alchemist experiences the joy and love found in relating to the psychoidal figures. As they marry, the alchemist marries both of them and from then on engages in discourse with both Sophia and God whenever the alchemist wishes. The alchemist knows the simple but infinite joy of loving and being loved by the two pillars of the incarnated godhead. He or she can talk with them or simply be with them, but in either case the experience fills his or her soul with delight and peace.

Moreover, the two united in one body generate a new light, a light that is tangible and substantial. The alchemist sees, feels, touches, and is touched by this light, and with its touch it ushers the alchemist into altered states of consciousness, or visions of profound insight, as he or she looks directly into the face of the sun and moon. I cannot hope to describe this light; nor the experience of it; it not only fills the mind and the soul but the body as well, and as you gaze upon it, you see the center of all that is. It is, in addition, not a weak vision, for the center has transformed itself into a house of solidity and strength, so that whoever beholds it sees clearly and without doubt and feels the heat of God entering every pore.

The Divine Pair feed the alchemist through ecstatic vision and love, and bestow Sophia's greatest gift: her wisdom. As an alchemist having reached this state, you would see yourself and your myth with clarity, and begin to perceive the soul of the entire world and everything in it. You would see the path that should be taken, and the path that is taken by all beings. You would gain the wisdom of your own Self and of the Self in all things. You would also gain the power to live your myth not in dreams or in visions, but in everyday life no matter how hard the struggle to actualize that myth. You would have the power to achieve it, if not in full, then in a part so great as to be infinitely rewarding. Finally, with all these gifts comes the knowledge that they are forever, that forever you will gaze on the light, will relate to your divine lovers and will study the ways of wisdom without end. The sense of immortality found everywhere in the *Aurora* is realized experientially and you come to know that death has no meaning. United with the soul of life, you do not fear death.

I am sure my descriptions fall far short of conveying what this union is like, but I wished to illustrate, if nothing else, that the union is real as are its fruits. Thomas does not write of symbolic truths alone, but of psychoidal ones that may be tasted and felt with as much clarity and depth as any experience of the ordinary world or the psychic one. We speak neither of dreams nor shadows, but of that which is most real.

THE PILLARS OF WISDOM'S HOUSE

Thomas states that the house is built on 14 pillars, and proceeds to describe each of these pillars in terms of their virtues and attributes. This section is at times confusing, for sometimes Thomas speaks of the Stone and sometimes of the alchemist. When he is speaking of the alchemist the comments are fairly simple, for they concern the more or less commonly stated virtues required of an alchemist in order to do the work. When he speaks of the Stone, his imagery is more complex and requires some explanation.

He describes the first pillar as health, for the Stone grants health to the one who uses it. The power of the Stone to heal is widely accepted, and I have referred to it more than once. He next describes the second pillar as humility, and quotes Pseudo-Aristotle as saying "With this Stone it is not good to fight."[11] The Stone bestows great gifts on the alchemists, and the *Aurora*'s previous parables have made clear that the alchemist helps the Stone come into being. But how does the alchemist relate to the Stone? Keep in mind that the Stone is a living thing, an entity, and not a possession. The alchemist relates to the Stone from the moment he begins his work to the time when he has created the Stone. In some ways this relationship is key to the successful conclusion of the *opus*. Little is said in the *Aurora* about this relationship. Here, however, Thomas tells the alchemist not to fight with the Stone.

Humility means that the alchemist must follow Wisdom and not try to control her. The great gifts of Wisdom are knowledge about the right place of things in the universe, about the right course of action, as well as the power to penetrate all things. As Boehme wrote, he who has the Stone can know all things on heaven and earth.[12] Clearly, he or she who has the Stone holds great power both to know and to influence. But this kind of knowing is outside the bonds of the human being, even of the Self. The individuated person, as well as the beginner in the process, must yield to the guidance of Wisdom. She or he who possesses the Stone and its power to heal may well wish to heal any and all she or he encounters; yet there are times when such healing is not allowed. Wisdom knows that a person must suffer for certain reasons and although, for instance, we may desire to end a loved one's pain, we must defer to Wisdom. It is the same with our own suffering. Possessing the Stone does not end suffering *per se*, or disease of the body, or conflict with others. Rather than using the power of the Stone to escape from the shadow side of life, we must have the humility to accept the darkness and work with it, trusting that the Stone gives us what is required. Humility therefore denotes the sacrifice of control, and that in relationship with Sophia the human partner defers and allows her to lead.

The third pillar is holiness, which means that the mind and soul of the alchemist have been purified and made holy, as the Stone is holy. Purity of mind has two meanings in this context. Thomas quotes Psalm 17 to the effect that "with the holy thou shalt be holy."[13] In other words, we must in ourselves be pure and holy in order to relate to the Stone that is holy. Again, Thomas seems to speak of the relationship between the alchemist and the Stone. But in what way may the alchemist be pure and holy? The most interesting reference Thomas makes in this regard is to the *Turba*, which he quotes as saying, "I have put my pleasures aside and prayed to God, that he would show me the pure water, which I know to be pure vinegar."[14] It is easy to understand that the alchemist must put his pleasures aside and pray to learn about the Stone, but what does vinegar have to do with being holy?

In alchemy, purity refers to the state in which all extraneous substances have been removed. Gold, for example, in its natural state is corrupted by the presence of matter that does not belong to it. Vinegar is acidic, and therefore a dissolving substance used to eradicate all the material that does not belong naturally to gold. Thus, vinegar is an agent that creates purity. If we apply this to the state of the alchemist, Thomas is saying that vinegar purifies the alchemist so that the relationship between the alchemist and the Stone may be established.

Since vinegar makes gold pure through its dissolving action, it likewise makes the alchemist pure by a process that removes anything that does not naturally belong to the alchemist's psyche. This would refer to collective material, the projections of other people, and the alchemist's false self-perceptions formed by the behavior of significant others such as parents. The psyche is purified therefore of all that does not belong to the Self. Purity in this sense means that the alchemist has achieved a good understanding of who he or she is and an ability to manifest that. It would therefore imply that she or he has accomplished a good deal of inner alchemy, or working on the Self psychologically and spiritually. The alchemist has achieved the second *coniunctio* in which the Self manifests and is pure enough to relate to the psychoidal Stone. Only by achieving the inward Stone can we discover the outward Stone. To paraphrase Gerald Dorn, unless you make yourself a stone first, you will never find the outer, or psychoidal, Stone. This is important because any impurities that distort the alchemist's perception of self will also distort perception of the Twin and will therefore create problems in the relationship. Notice, however, that making yourself the Stone is not

the final stage, but opens the door to psychoidal alchemy wherein you discover the Holy Twin. In short, holiness requires that the alchemist has
achieved his or her own transformation before attempting the transformation of Wisdom. It also means that the relationship between the alchemist
and the Stone is one of equal partners, both of whom are holy, but humility requires that this equality be a qualified one.

The next pillar is that of chastity, which makes sense on the face of it as
a Christian virtue. But all the references Thomas makes are alchemical and
are worth giving in full:

> Whom when I love I am pure, (when I touch I am chaste); whose
> mother is a virgin and whose father hath not cohabited [sic]with
> her, for he is fed upon virgin's milk, etc. Wherefore Avicenna saith
> in the Mineralis: Certain learned ones use a water, which is called
> virgin's milk.[15]

This quote is not an easy one to interpret. It seems that chastity has to do
with the relationship between Sophia and her lover. I would say that Sophia
is speaking and that she says that she finds chastity in the touch of her lover.
Loving God and being in relationship with the holy is chastity. Loving God
and entering into such relationship is itself transformative and creates the
chastity necessary for the relationship, itself. The touch of God makes
Sophia's love pure or chaste for the simple reason that God is chaste.

The "he" referred to by Thomas is therefore God. Chastity and lack of
contamination are true both of God and of Sophia and mark them as divine
rather than human beings. Their love is naturally divine and therefore
chaste. Furthermore, the child to whom they give birth, the *filius
philosophorum*, is also chaste for it is born of their love. The *filius* is chaste
also because it is born from a mother who is a virgin and from a father who
has had no sex with her, for their union is miraculous. The divine birth of
the *filius* provides another comparison between him and Christ. Von Franz
found an interesting parallel to our quotation in the writings of Ephraem
Syrus, whose Christian hymn says, "Let the earth praise him [Christ], who
with her waters nourishes the fruits and adores the sun, and looks upon the
pure child who sucks the virgin's milk."[16] As she says, the reference to virgin's milk equates the *filius* with Christ and reveals once more that the *filius*
is both divine and the son of the divine.

Chastity thus refers to Sophia, God, and their children. It also can refer
to the alchemist. Though human, and clearly not of a virgin birth, the
alchemist finds chastity in loving Sophia in the same way that God and

Sophia find chastity in their mutual love. The perfection that chastity implies belongs to the divine, not to the human, but union between the human and the divine allows the human partner to experience something of his or her beloved's chastity. The holiness and the sanctity of the alchemist come not from his or her virtue or efforts; it comes from loving and being loved by the divine. Loving Wisdom is holiness, chastity, and perfection. Being in relationship with Sophia allows the alchemist to experience something precious that can be gained in no other way.

Thomas now moves to a discussion about the Philosopher's Stone and Its attribute of virtue. As he uses the term, virtue is power. In alchemy, virtue is not a moral attribute but refers instead to the essence of a thing. The virtue of sulfur, for example, is the power that sulfur has to form substances and this power derives from its essence. Virtue is a power or ability to manifest in a certain way. Herbs, metals, and all natural things have their own virtue, which is not in their body but in the spirit contained within their body. Thus, the power must be brought forth with the spirit, or infused from above, as if the power of the stars were added to the earthy substance, thereby increasing its powers. As spirit is infused into the Stone, the latter undergoes fermentation and its powers noticeable increase.

Through alchemical processes, the virtues of heaven and earth are incarnated in the *filius* or the Stone. Thomas writes, "And it receiveth the virtue of the upper and lower planets,"[17] and later he quotes the *Book of Quintessence*: "for I could not wonder enough at the great virtue of the thing, which is bestowed upon and infused into it from heaven."[18]

This image, like the last, illustrates the multiplication of the power of the Stone by feeding it spiritual energy and power, which causes it to develop and evolve to a higher state of being and power. It is a motif worth repeating, for it is the principle work of psychoidal alchemy. We must find the entity with which we are to work. We then realize that the entity, however powerful in its own right, is tainted and unformed; a shadow of what it could become if it were brought into relationship with its source and with the ally. This stage of the work requires feeding it divine energies and powers, not that it might grow strong for its own sake, but that in growing strong it gains the ability to meet its partner and unite with it. This is paralleled in the human being who must grow strong enough to resist being swept away by the powers of the psychoid. So, too, a figure like Sophia must transform and be purified so that she takes on her true nature and power. The addition of power to Sophia occurs in two forms. Her marriage to the masculine image of God is a union with the divine power, and the addition of the spiritual forces to their union multiplies their power and essence as well.

These two processes act as one of the pillars of the house that Sophia built. The alchemist must discover within him- or herself the ability to see the virtue of the spirit, to "grasp" this spirit, and feed it to Sophia. This is one of the great mysteries of alchemy and cannot be taught, for it must evolve with the powers of the alchemist and with those of the Stone.

The sixth pillar of the house of Wisdom is victory. Thomas quotes Hermes as saying that the Stone shall be victorious over every solid thing and precious stone, then switches back to theology and quotes the apocalypse: "To him that overcometh I will give the subtle hidden manna and a new name which the mouth of the Lord hath named."[19] And then he refers back to alchemy, for he says that when the Stone of victory comes into being it can create metals, jaspers, and chrysolites that surpass the natural. It is always fascinating to watch Thomas weave alchemy and theology together, as he searches for the image to convey the experience he describes.

The Stone of victory can penetrate and conquer all solid things and every precious stone—this ability is by now familiar to us. In addition, however, the Stone of victory receives a new name pronounced by the mouth of the Lord.

Naming is of the greatest importance, for in the name of a thing lays its original nature and essential being. There are many references to naming in alchemy, and the alchemists seem to have great fun naming mysterious substances, or calling the Stone by a hundred different names. Yet the true name spoken by the Lord is something else again. Edward Kelly quotes Rhasis ("Book of Lights") as saying that, "Our Stone is named after the creation of the world, being three and yet one."[20] Another alchemists explains, "Tis a grand point to discover the true material, which is the subject of our work; & one must needs to that end pierce the thousand dark veils, wherewith it is enwrapped; one . . . must distinguish it by its own proper name."[21] In other words, the Stone's own name is hidden by the multiplicity of names used in alchemy. Its name denotes its nature, and whoever discovers the name discovers the thing so named. Penetrating the veils of mystery, we see into the true essence of the thing itself.

The name, if it is true, is the same as that which is named. But Thomas says that the Stone of victory receives a new name from the very mouth of God. This indicates a transformation that occurs from the original state to that of being the Stone, a change so profound that the very name of the entity is altered. In this case, Sophia receives the new name, which would have to be *filius*, indicating the change she has undergone by experiencing the *coniunctio*. She receives her name from the mouth of God, presumably by the lover she weds. In wedding the masculine aspect of God she receives from him a new essence, that of the ally, and it might equally be said that He receives a new essence as well. Together they form that which is greater than either.

The seventh and eighth pillars are hope and faith, which Thomas equates with believing in that which we cannot see. This marks a return to the perspective of the alchemist who must believe in the Stone even before it comes into being, for, "It is invisible like unto the soul in man's body."[22] This refers to the living fire or the spirit before it manifests in the body. Little more need be said about these two components, but in the next pillar we come upon a topic of great interest and importance.

The ninth pillar is charity, which Thomas speaks of as love. Alchemy seems often devoid of feelings, but feeling is essential in psychoidal alchemy, for it is the love between God and Sophia and of both for their human partner that makes the work possible or even desirable. Those who seek the ally or the Stone for their own gain fail, but those who seek it for love can never fail. At whatever stage of the work they arrive at, they will find fulfillment in love. Thomas is speaking now of the alchemist, but likely also of Sophia, for both feel love for each other. He makes it obvious that love is of primary importance in a selection of ecclesiastical quotes that are applied to the work: I love them that love me. Here it is Sophia speaking as she promises to love any who come to her in love, and the "proof of love is the display of the work."[23]

Those who love do the work. Those who do the work do so for love. Anyone who has even imagined working with psychoidal figures or penetrating the mysteries of union with such figures knows that success requires not only grace, but also the greatest of efforts. Thomas also quotes King Alphonsus, who said, "This is a true friend who deserteth thee not when all the world faileth thee."[24] Such is the devotion required of us when we do psychoidal alchemy, for as I have shown, there are few in our world who take spirit seriously, and even fewer who love and work with figures of the psychoid. As Sophia earlier complained, all desert her and the wisdom of the world denies the existence of Wisdom itself, so that it takes a brave soul to buck collective opinion and do this work. Moreover, it takes sacrifice, for not only does the work require time and energy, it demands that the alchemist forbear control and learn to let the visionary world direct his or her every step. The alchemist does not control the process, nor can he or she direct it to his or her own goals. Instead, God and Sophia have their own agenda: union with each other, and nothing less than that suffices.

If necessary, the alchemist must give up his or her own plans and ambitions to seek the goal of the *coniunctio*: "All that a man hath will he give for his soul, that is for this stone."[25] This is not a work for the weak-willed or the faint of heart; we must be willing to give up everything for the sake of the Stone or we shall most likely fail. It is very popular these days to emphasize the need for grace, and it is true that we need the help of the inner and psychoidal entities to perform this work. Yet, as Sophia said, those that love her, she loves, and love is in the work. We must win the love of Sophia and of the ally by doing the necessary work, for though they both love from the beginning, they neither can nor will give themselves away cheaply. In my years of teaching, I have witnessed many students drop out and give up the work when the going got tough. Somehow they, and many like them, assume that good intention is the same as accomplishment, or that the spirits owe them something. The work is hard, the rewards are great, but only love supplies the courage and the dedication to see the work through the difficult times. As Thomas concludes, "For he who soweth sparingly shall also reap sparingly; and he who is not a partaker of the sufferings shall not be of the consolation."[26]

The tenth pillar is goodness, of which little is said by Thomas, and the eleventh is patience. Patience is another of those hard-to-come-by virtues that are required for the work, for nothing in alchemy moves quickly. It may take years to develop our Self, and years more to learn to perceive the psychoid. Manifestation of the ally does not come quickly, nor does the marriage with Sophia occur over night. We cannot be discouraged by the length of the journey, but must learn patience. This is not always hard, for there are many stages on the way filled with delight, and it would be tempting to linger there for as long as possible if necessity did not drive us forward. But there are other times when all is confusion and the ally seems lost, and Wisdom hidden in obscurity, when, with faith and hope, we do what we can and wait for the results. Morienus says, "He who hath not patience, let him hold back his hand from the work."[27] In other words, if you do not have the patience to work through all that needs to be done it is better not to start. For starting is a commitment, and broken commitments are never healthy.

The twelfth pillar is temperance, and with this one Thomas shifts our attention once more from the alchemist to the Stone, itself. Temperance is a

guide to the work, for the four elements coming together in harmony create the Stone:

> For temperance is a mixture of the elements one with another,
> such that the warm is tempered with the cold, the dry with the
> humid; and the philosophers have been most careful to insist that
> one may not exceed another, saying: Beware lest the secret escape,
> beware lest the vinegar be changed into smoke, beware lest ye put
> to flight the king and his consort with too much fire, beware of all
> that is beyond the mean, but place it on the fire of corruption, that
> is of temperance, until they are joined of their own accord.[28]

One of the many secrets of alchemy is balance, and many schools of
alchemy have insisted that the right balance between the elements, or
between the fire and the Stone, determines the success of the work. George
Ripley urges the alchemist to leave the matter to its own work during which
it undergoes processes that let its components harmonize and become "pro-
moted unto a most perfect temperance."[29]

Temperance creates harmony between the components of the alchemical work. In psychoidal alchemy, temperance requires that the psychoidal
entity harmonize itself, first with the alchemist, so that it does not over-
whelm or injure him or her, and then within itself, so that it comes to the
right balance of body, soul, and spirit. The body transforms into the light
body of the ally, and the soul purified of all imperfections becomes the
essential expression of individuality, while the spirit is stimulated into activity that supports and drives the processes of transformation. Finally, the
psychoidal entity must harmonize its partner, creating the marriage that
binds them together as *filius*. The alchemist must be temperate by developing patience and love, and the psychoidal being is temperate by coming into
harmony with itself, its partner, and then with the ally.

The thirteenth pillar is in many ways the most important. Thomas calls
it spiritual understanding. "If ye understand in the spirit, ye shall also know
the spirit.... O how many understand not the sayings of the wise; these have
perished because of their foolishness, for they lacked spiritual understanding and found nothing in toil."[30]Alchemists of every time and place insist
that only through spiritual understanding can their writings make sense. As
Titus Burckhardt wrote:

> Another reason why alchemical doctrine hides itself in riddles is
> because it is not meant for everyone. The "royal art" presupposes a

more than ordinary understanding, and also a certain cast of soul, failing which its practice may involve no small dangers for the soul.[31]

The "more than ordinary understanding" is something of an understatement. There are many ways in which understanding, or Wisdom, comes into play in alchemy, especially psychoidal alchemy. The secrets of alchemy lie in the interaction of spirit and matter, and, in psychoidal alchemy, the union of psychoidal energies and agencies that are manifested as personages. In our understanding of alchemy, we must be able to see beyond the literal meaning of the words of the texts in order to comprehend that, on the one hand, alchemy is a symbolic system describing the inner workings of the psyche, and, on the other, that alchemy is a description not of gold, metals, or of ordinary nature, but of cosmic forces and powers. Joseph Needham, in his seminal work on Chinese science and alchemy, wrote that "the dominant goal of proto-scientific alchemy was contemplative, and indeed the language in which the Elixir is described was ecstatic."[32] Needham also believed that alchemy was concerned with cosmic principles and events that were duplicated in the body or in the laboratory:

> The alchemist undertook to contemplate the cycles of cosmic process in their newly accessible form [those found in the reaction-vessel] because he believed that to encompass the Tao with his mind (or, as he would have put it, his mind-and-heart) would make him one with it. That belief was precisely what made him a Taoist.[33]

Alchemy in both the East and West saw underneath the surface events to the cosmic reality they portrayed. Where common understanding sees only the outward shape of things, alchemical understanding sees the play of forces that are often invisible. Yet alchemical wisdom is not that of the invisible forces, for as Neeedham points out, they contemplate these cosmic forces made newly accessible. All alchemy is, in this sense, concerned with the psychoid, for it attempts to bring the cosmic forces into a semi-physical form so that alchemists may interact with them as well as observe them. In psychoidal alchemy, these forces embody themselves as figures and personalities, and only an uncommon understanding can see them and interact with them. Normal understanding dismisses the idea of cosmic forces altogether, or if it accepts them, rejects the idea that they may be made substantial and so understood through the senses. To perceive the psychoid and to behold the mysteries of the divinity and of the world incarnate in beings that are autonomous and relational requires a most uncommon understanding, indeed.

Thomas's discussion of the last pillar speaks of obedience and the need to follow the teachings of the wise. All may agree with this without much discussion, and on this rather flat note he moves to the end of the parable. He concludes by saying once more that this is the house that Wisdom founded, but then goes on to add the interesting comment that the four and twenty elders can open this house with the keys of the kingdom of heaven. In short, this is a heavenly house. Von Franz interprets the saying when she writes that the "whole edifice [is] comparable to the 'kingdom of heaven'; in other words, he beholds in an intuitive vision a crystallization of the self in the world beyond."[34] On one hand, her comment is very appropriate and accurate. On the other, I have argued that the house Sophia built is really a psychoidal house. However, it is important to keep in mind that the psychoidal house embodies an aspect of the heavenly world. If we recall our threefold division of the universe into ordinary world, psychoid world, and the world of spirit beyond our perception, von Franz's insight reminds us that Sophia includes within herself aspects of this unknown, spiritual reality. Though the house has been built within the psychoid world and is thereby an incarnation of Wisdom, we must remember that Wisdom contains within Herself mysteries that we may never perceive. In this sense, we can say that the house is an intuitive perception of the unknown world of spirit as long as we remember that we can experience the house as a psychoidal reality and not simply as an intuitive perception.

We need to emphasize the difference between a psychoidal experience and an intuitive one in order to highlight that psychoidal alchemy deals with forces made visible and quasi-physical so that we can truly touch and know them. Wisdom has reached the stage in this parable of being incarnate in the body of light, but it is important to remember that despite the fact that we can experience Sophia as a psychoidal entity, she carries within her nature a mystery we can never comprehend. This is a truly marvelous paradox: we can touch and feel Sophia and even marry her, knowing all the time that heaven lies within her beyond the scope of our knowledge. I have emphasized in my interpretation of this parable the miraculous adventure of her becoming solid and substantial, thereby offering us the ability to experience her in hitherto unimaginable ways. Yet, she remains forever an incomprehensible and delectable mystery.

OF HEAVEN AND EARTH:
INCARNATION AND IMMORTALITY

In the penultimate chapter of the *Aurora*, Thomas speaks once more of the mysteries of the earth and of the spirit. Earth is the dominant theme, for we are facing two mysteries: the incarnation of Wisdom in her newly transformed body, and the mystery of immortality through which the earth, or the body, becomes permanent and eternal. This difficult text concerns some of the deepest ideas found in alchemy, but, given our work as we traveled through the previous ten parables, we are in a position to understand what Thomas writes about.

It is clear by now that Thomas exalts the earth and the body to its highest position throughout the *Aurora*. This reveals his fascination with the immortal body and with the incarnation of the spirit. From the psychoidal perspective, Thomas is struggling to express the idea that spiritual beings take on form, and thereby belong to the psychoid. The earth is the form that they take on, as well as the quasi-material substance to which the form molds itself. The soul is the individual nature of a spiritual being and it expresses itself in the form that the body assumes, while the universal spirit empowers and enlivens that new form so that it lives forever. As Wisdom gains her immortality in the psychoid realm, her human partner, the alchemist, also takes on immortality. The alchemist, too, changes form, putting off the old mortal form and putting on the new immortal one. Having done the inner work, the alchemist also knows his or her essential nature and individuality to which he or she gives expression in the new form, and also is endowed with spiritual forces and powers.

In this parable of heaven and earth, Thomas once more describes the processes of creating the new earth and its relationship with heaven, that is, with the spiritual forces and powers. In this case, von Franz's understanding of this parable is excellent and must be consulted before we continue. She believes that this whole parable concerns an alchemical world-creating process that centers on the image of the earth, which she believes symbolizes the feminine deity. She goes on to say that from this deity a new cosmos blossoms forth. Thus, "We can easily recognize the 'earth' as the anima-Wisdom figure of the earlier chapters, but now she is purified and spiritualized."[1] In other words, the earth is Sophia incarnate in her new body, and from her a whole new cosmos emerges. There are traditions that teach that one's union with spirits generates a world or universe unique to one and one's spirit. This is certainly true in the Sufi tradition. In the theories of Avicenna, spiritual forces take on the form and appearance of angels, and there is one special angel for each human being. If the human being unites with his or her angel, both escape from the shared universe and discover one of their own. Each angel has its own world, its own reality, and through union with this angel the human and the angel are freed from any world but their own. Henry Corbin explains this in his usually challenging but wonderful way:

> The celestial kinship of the soul is declared in a simple fact whose implication is twofold: it is by awakening to consciousness of itself, by attaining to consciousness of self, that the soul is enabled to know the Angel and the world of the Angel, and, by thus attaining the "clime of the angel"—that is, the *Orient*—is *eo ipso* enabled to realize its exodus from the cosmos that is the Occident—that is, to affirm its transcendence in respect to that cosmos . . . transcendence in respect to sensible space does not imply evanescence into the *formless* or the unfigurable. Pure *Forms* have an intelligible "space" of their own.[2]

In other words, psychoidal beings have their own space that is different from ordinary space; in fact, they have their own worlds to which their human partner goes. In this sense, Sophia, as earth, may create her own cosmos. Therefore, the earth is Sophia who is capable, as an angelic or psychoidal force, of generating a new world based on her own essence, and of carrying her alchemist partner into that world. But her new world is no less of form than our world; it is simply different from ours. Keeping this model in mind, let us now look at the parable in question.

The parable opens with, "He that is of the earth, of the earth he speaketh, he that cometh from heavens is above all."[3] He that comes from the heavens is the masculine aspect of God representing the higher worlds of the spirit. He is both of the earth and of the heavens, but the earth is the "principle and mother of the other elements."[4] The mother of all is Sophia, so that in the first paragraph we have earth as Sophia and heaven as the world of God. Both are of the psychoid, but Sophia represents the feminine force of generation and creation, while God embodies the heavenly powers.

Thomas launches into a discussion of the processes by which God and Sophia unite and through which a new world is made. He first equates the human being with the earth, for man is ashes, and to ashes he will return. But, as you might expect, ash is a powerful alchemical image. Thomas wrote that such ashes, into which man has returned, are mixed with the permanent water, which is "the ferment of gold, and their gold is the body, that is the earth. . . . It is the earth of the Promised Land, wherein Hermes commanded his son to sow gold, that living rains might ascend from it."[5]

In trying to make sense of this statement, it is useful to begin with the image of ashes. To leave our Western tradition for a moment, ashes in Hindu alchemy are part of the divine essence through which a new universe is generated. Shiva says of ashes that they are "my seed, and I bear my own seed upon my body. . . . Let a man smear his body until it is pale with ashes. . . . Then he attains the status of Lord of the Host . . . and grasps the supreme ambrosia."[6] Ashes are the fertilizing and creative power that transforms a human being into a god. In Western alchemy they are of equal importance.

Paracelsus, for example, believed in the creative and fertilizing power of ashes:

> If the living bird be burned to dust and ashes in a sealed cucurbite with the third degree of fire, and then, still shut up, be putrefied with the highest degree of putrefaction in a *venter equinus* so as to become a mucilaginous phlegm, then that phlegm can again be brought to maturity, and so, renovated and restored, can become a living bird, provided the phlegm be once more enclosed in its jar or receptacle. This is to revive the dead by regeneration and clarification, which is indeed a great and profound miracle of Nature. By this process all birds can be killed and again made to live, to be renovated and restored. This is the very greatest and highest miracle and mystery of God. . . .[7]

In other words, the ashes of the dead bird, putrified, can be brought back to life as the living bird. One sees this imagery in *The Chemical Wedding of*

Christian Rosenkreutz, where the bodies of the king and queen are reduced to ashes out of which arises a wondrous bird, which in turn is killed. From its ashes, mixed with blood, the king and queen are restored to life.

As Jung pointed out, ash is the "diadem of the heart" and the "pure foliated earth" and seems to be related to the glorified body purified of all the "darkness of the soul, and of the black matter, for the wickedness of base earthiness has been separated from it."[8] The ash is the residue of the body that has undergone severe purgation and purification; it is therefore the most pure aspect of the body to which the soul is added in order to create the glorified body, or the Philosopher's Stone. When, therefore, Thomas asks that the ashes be mixed with the permanent water he is saying take the purified body that is free of taint and mix it with—what? The permanent water is another key symbol in understanding this process.

Alchemists often relate their permanent water to divine water, which dissolves the body into itself and unites with it, so that the water becomes earth as well, or the earth becomes water. This water perfects the body, allowing it to become the stone.[9] The original form is lost in the water, in preparation for the generation of the new form. However, in working with alchemy we must realize that there are many levels of the work, and that the same image can have different meanings at the different levels. By the time matter has been reduced to ashes, the form no longer exists. The water does not at this level serve to destroy form, but to create it by the union of itself and the ashes. The seed has already germinated when ash and water are brought together to create the higher form:

> The secret of our Art is the union of man and woman: the husband receives the tingeing spirit from his wife. The union of husband and wife coagulates the female principle; and if the whole be transmuted into red, we have the treasure of the world, of which Synon says: "If the water be changed into the body, the body is changed, first into earth, then into dust and ashes, and you have what you want.[10]

In short, in the union of the ashes and the water we have an image of the *coniunctio*. The ashes refer to the body of the Stone, formed through the incarnation of Sophia, and the water is the spirit, now related to the power of heaven or to God. Sophia, once brought into her perfected form, is united with the purified God in order to create the Stone. In this parable, earth becomes Sophia and spirit becomes God, as the two now embody the most perfect expression of their being. Both body and spirit are elevated to their highest form and united. The highest form of body is Sophia and the highest form of spirit is God. The union of water and ash indicates a preliminary union of God and Sophia, and points the way to the final union that will complete the work. I say "preliminary union" because ash and water are not personified beings, and it is only at the level of personified beings that the final union is completed. One sees this repeatedly in alchemy, for the work is never accomplished until the king is transformed, or the king and queen married, or the prince and the king reunited. The final *coniunctio* always takes place with images that are personified.

The union that occurs at the level of elements or substances is never complete. So in this chapter of the *Aurora*, we have the symbolic union of heaven and earth, but that union gives way to the ecstatic union portrayed in the next chapter. There are thus stages to the process of union that lead to the final consummation.

The work on the Stone is never complete. It can always grow and develop, no matter what level it has reached. It must die in a certain sense every time it grows, so that, as in the parable of heaven and earth, it is once more ash. But ash is not just the image for the reduction of form, it is the symbol of the divine core of soul and body, that which can be reduced no further. The unified Stone is the ash, for it is the divine body and the divine soul as one. But united with the universal spirit which first gave birth to it, it experiences yet more development and transformation.

The permanent water is therefore the universal spirit and is essentially the same as the fire. Fire first created the ashes, so it is the first operation of the spirit on body and soul, while water unites with the ash in order to become a body itself. In the previous parts of this book we have seen the Stone form through the union of body and soul; now the spirit, universal and impersonal, becomes one with the Stone as well. The universal and impersonal spirit becomes particular and personal by becoming personified in the psychoid as the masculine partner of Sophia. Divine energies are now channeled into the union with Sophia, creating yet a new level of development as she absorbs and becomes one with this spirit. It is for this reason that the parable is titled "Of Heaven and Earth," for it deals with the union of the heavenly spirit and the glorified body. In this process all three components of the Stone—body, soul, and spirit—are fully united.

The permanent water, Thomas goes on to say, is the ferment of gold, and "their gold is the body, that is the earth, which Aristotle called the coagulant, since it cogulateth water. It is the earth of the Promised Land. . ."[11] The body of the Promised Land is the glorified body in the last parable of the *Aurora*, and it is a magical body that operates to coagulate water, or the ferment. Ferment is related to the soul and is the process by which the soul impresses its form upon the *prima materia*. Lyndy Abraham says of the ferment that it is during this stage that the soul and "purified body are chemically and permanently joined together."[12] Thus, we have in the ferment yet another image of union between Sophia and her consort. This description still occurs at the elemental level and not at the personified level, so it is still incomplete; yet it marks another stage in the permanent joining of masculine and feminine aspects of the divinity.

Thomas has written of this unitive process several times now and in many different fashions; it is a difficult process to comprehend. He has previously written of the union of the body, soul, and spirit, but as the union moves toward its culminating point, he describes it as the union of heaven and earth. Keeping in mind that heaven is God and all of his powers and earth is Sophia with all of her receptivity and creativity, the union of heaven and earth is profound. In order to give some idea of how profound Thomas believed this union to be, I quote from him at length:

> [T]he earth moved and the heavens are poured out upon it, and they flow as if with honey throughout all the world and tell its glory. For this glory is now only to him who hath understanding, how of the earth the heavens were made, and therefore the earth remaineth for ever and the heavens are founded upon it. . . . The deep is its clothing, above it shall stand water, air, fire, and the birds of the air shall swell therein, watering it from the upper elements, that it may be filled with the fruit of their works, because in the center of the earth these seven planets took root, and left their virtues there. . . . This earth, I say, made the moon in its season, then the sun arose . . . all things serve the earth, and the days of its years are threescore and ten years passing over it, but cause it to upholdeth all things by the word of its godhead. . . .[13]

Note initially the amazing role played by the earth, a role defying reason unless understood correctly. How could the earth make the heavens and the moon? How does the earth have a godhead? The answer is that the earth is Sophia, and as such is the creative expression of the divinity. She is the creator of all, and interestingly makes the moon before the sun. The moon is *luna*, or the feminine principle, and the sun is *sol*, or the masculine principle. According to Thomas, Sophia makes the feminine principle before the masculine, an idea not often found in the Christian world. The feminine principle is given first place because Sophia creates all things—even, it seems, her spouse.

The following quotation plays on the incest motif in alchemy in some startling ways. The most significant image is that of putting the mother in the womb of her child after she, herself, has given birth to the child. Sophia creates her children, from whom she is born and with whom she unites. Alchemically, Sophia is the mercury, or *prima materia*, that first gives forth matter, and then she is the divine force placed within the matter and brought forth from it once more. The alchemical mercury, here correlated with Sophia, creates, enters creation, emerges, and unites with creation in turn:

> It is the royal fountain in which the king and queen bathe themselves; and the mother must be put into and sealed up within the belly of her infant . . . who proceed from her, and whom she brought forth; and therefore they have loved one another as mother and son, and are conjoined together, because they come from one and the same root, and are of the same substance and nature.[14]

From the perspective of psychoidal alchemy, Sophia is the mother of all the psychoidal forces and places herself within them to take on their attributes or virtues. As she emerges from them as the liberated spirit, she takes with her all their powers, adding them to the power of the ally.

As the first creative principle of all things, Sophia is the earth out of which arises moon and sun and stars. United to her own children, she transforms and becomes first the ally, and then adds to herself the power of the stars, or the heavenly virtues. Thomas says that in the center of the earth the seven planets took root, and then left their virtues there. Within the earth, within the form of the Great Mother, lie all powers and virtues. This description refers to the process I described earlier when the stars, or psychoidal forces, were made part of Sophia; it emphasizes the great power of Sophia as earth, and the great power of the conjunction by which heaven and earth become one thing. Notice that in addition to the infusion of the heavenly power through the union of earth and heaven, the other psychoidal forces are now part of this union by their appearance within the womb of Sophia. God as husband brings power with him, but so do the other psychoidal beings as they find their proper place within the being of Sophia. These miracles are repeated in the experience of the psychoidal alchemist who is able to conjoin Sophia and her spouse, after first allowing the separation of the soul and the body of Sophia.

Since the alchemist experiences this in his or her own work, there is a tremendous impact upon him or her by the conjunction. The alchemist joined to Sophia and subsequently to the ally experiences immortality, for at the moment of conjunction "this mortal [the alchemist] shall put on immortality, and the corruption of the living shall put on incorruption, then indeed shall that word come to pass which is written, Death is swallowed up by victory. O death, where is thy victory?"[15]

Thomas has returned to the theme of immortality repeatedly, and this is the reward of the alchemist who succeeds in creating the union of Sophia and her son-lover, who infuses the earth with all the powers of heaven. In whatever way we might understand this idea, there is no doubt that the alchemist experiences a profound transformation when the conjunction is achieved. I have not emphasized this transformation, for my focus has been on what has happened to the psychoidal entities, but it must never be forgotten that the human being witnessing and abetting this union within the divinity is profoundly and eternally changed.

Through the union of Sophia and God, the second Adam is created who heals the wound created by the fall of the first Adam, for the second Adam, who is "called the philosophic man,"[16] is eternal and passes on this gift of eternity to all men. With this statement, Thomas returns to the other major theme of the work—the universal redemption of humankind and nature. In the conjunction of the masculine and the feminine, of the son and his mother, and the subsequent creation of the *filius*, all things are restored to purity and eternity. Thomas closes on a typical alchemical note of making earth water, and water air, and so on, which refers to the union of opposites and the production of the quintessence, or the matter of the Stone. In the next chapter of the *Aurora*, the union of opposites becomes the sacred marriage between the two lovers.

CHAPTER 11

THE LOVER WITH THE BELOVED:
THE WEDDING OF SOPHIA

For many reasons this is the most moving and profound of the parables of the *Aurora*. It describes the final stage of the work, when the mystical marriage takes place, and it reflects the love and ecstasy that we can experience at this stage. From the depths of the heart come expressions of devotion and commitment, and of the joy that lovers know. The mystic marriage is the joining of the two poles of the divinity itself, and of the divine and the human.

Sophia has transformed. Her soul, her individuality, removed from her old form, underwent purification of such depth that it appeared as cosmic renewal. It was then reincarnated in a form, a psychoidal body of light, at one with its divine lover. To this *rebis* was then added the spiritual virtues or powers of the psychoid realm, and the whole coagulated into a new being. What remains is for the soul of God and the soul of Sophia to pledge themselves to each other in eternal embrace, becoming two though one, one though two. The expressions of love are between them; the psychoidal alchemist shares in the bliss of this union as witness and companion. In this parable, therefore, Thomas tries to find the words to express the *mysterium coniunctionis*.

He begins as if recapitulating the process: "Be turned to me with all your heart and do not cast me aside because I am black and swarthy, because the sun hath changed my colour, and the waters have covered my face and the earth hath been polluted . . ."[1] Sophia reminds her lover that she has been defiled, that the Earth, herself, has been polluted. She goes on to restate her loneliness and her despair, and at that moment in the text, the voice switches to the masculine:

> For behold in my bed by night I sought one to comfort me and I found none, I called and there was none to answer me. Therefore will I arise and go into the city, seeking in the streets and broad ways a chaste virgin to espouse, comely in face, more comely in body most comely in her garments, that she may roll back the stone from my sepulcher and give me wings like a dove, and I will fly with her into heaven. . . .[2]

The virgin whom he finds then reminds her lover of her stain and her imperfections. The psychoidal entity that is not in union with her lover is stained by its isolation and self-will. But the lover, the male voice, responds that he, too, has been imperfect, for without Sophia he has suffered intense isolation and loneliness. Thus the drama unfolds within the manifesting godhead. First the divinity emanates a feminine expression of itself, but almost in the act of emanation occurs an act of separation, and the masculine aspect of God must seek his feminine counterpart from whom he has been separated. Therefore he, too, is imperfect until he finds his wholeness in her. Notice that he proclaims she will give him wings and save him from his own grave. He is dead without Sophia. Only the cementing of the divine poles brings God as an individual, psychoidal form to full life and spiritual power.

"I will fly with her into heaven. . . . I live for ever, and will rest in her, for she [the queen] stood on my right hand in gilded clothing, surrounded with variety."[3] Sophia, the queen, is the feminine principle of life. Like the Shekinah in the Kabbalah, she is the queen of heaven and earth, the goddess as partner with god, the underlying feminine principle that gives life to the universe with her soul.

In another reversal typical of the paradoxical nature of alchemy, the king now calls Sophia his daughter, as he was her son, and the incest motif is referred to again as he desires his daughter for his lover. Sophia as the matrix is the mother of all things, including the psychoidal form of God, but God is the first emanator of all psychoidal beings. Therefore, he is father to them all. Thus, he is father to Sophia who nevertheless is his equal and his bride.

In the next section it is possible to imagine that the alchemist is talking, for he requires from Sophia a number of gifts. But I do not believe that this is the case. It is rather a continuation of the motif of God needing his feminine consort to be whole, so that the gifts she bestows upon him are aspects of this wholeness. He says to her:

Make known to me my end and what is the number of my days, that I may know what is wanting to me, for thou hast made all my days measurable and my substance is as nothing before thee. For thou art she who shall enter through the ear, through my domain, and I shall be clothed with a purple garment from thee and from me, and I will come forth as a bridegroom out of this bride-chamber . . .[4]

Sophia *knows* God, knows the ally. Knowing the number of His days and what is wanting to Him, making His days measurable and knowing His substance are important images of Sophia as Wisdom. For she is the mirror of the divinity and knows every aspect of His being, and one of the great gifts she bestows on Him is self-knowledge. I have spoken much of the many traditions in which God seeks self-knowledge and creates in order to know. His major aid in this process is His mirror who reflects Himself back to Himself, and this is Sophia. The human partner is necessary in this process, as the alchemist is necessary to the *coniunctio*, but Sophia is God's self-reflection.

In order to understand the immense power of Sophia's gift we must dissuade ourselves from holding the idea that God is perfect and omnipotent. He is not; He is in the process of becoming. Part of His becoming is the embracing of a unique psychoidal form, which partly entails His union with a human being and partly His becoming self-aware. It is through the marriage with Sophia that He accomplishes the latter. In my experience, this is not an all-or-nothing experience, but an evolutionary process whereby God gains knowledge of different aspects of His being and of creation through the process He engages in with His spouse. The marriage sets the stage for the on-going evolution of God. This is possible because Sophia is the personification of divine knowing.

The unusual image of entering through the ear is explained well by von Franz, who points out its relationship to the motif of the Holy Ghost entering through Mary's ear when she conceived Jesus. She quotes St. Isaac of Antioch who says that "unless [Christ] were God, how could he enter through the ear? . . . For by the ear the spirit entered and out of the womb issued the flesh."[5] Von Franz comments that this image indicates that the *coniunctio* was "simultaneously an incarnation of the Logos or of God, thereby expressing the spiritual and supernatural nature of the coniunctio."[6] The image obviously has to do with incarnation, and the events in question are supernatural. But Sophia enters into the God's ear; the mascu-

line is made pregnant by the feminine. This gift of Sophia allows God to give
birth to Himself as a more substantial being.

I have said often that the psychoid has a body, and that this body is not
spiritual form alone, but is substantial because the psychoid is the union of
spirit and matter. Yet the body has been seen to undergo transformation as
Sophia has repeatedly experienced alchemical processes. Now she alters the
body of God, but helping Him to incarnate in a new form, a form I earlier
called the ally, that is the unified being that resulted from the wedding of
Sophia and God. The new being has more tangible substance than the others previously had. There are degrees of substantiality within the psychoid,
and the more the entity incarnates, the more substance it assumes.
Experientially, the ally born of the wedding of Sophia and God has more
substance than either of the other two, and assumes the quality of light. As
this process goes on, the ally becomes more accessible, more visible, and
more powerful. The result of the marriage is the further incarnation of God,
and this incarnation does not only occur once, but is itself a process of
increasing manifestation and tangibility.

The bridegroom now is clothed with a "purple garment from thee and
from me," and He comes forth as the bridegroom from His bride-chamber.
Purple is the color of royalty, and in alchemy was often used as a synonym for
the red color of the elixir or final stage of the Stone. In Basil Valentine's writing, the Stone, itself, as teacher and guide, is an old man "of venerable age,
with snowy locks and silvery beard, and arrayed in a flowing purple robe. On
his head he wore a crown set with brilliant carbuncles. His loins were girded
with the girdle of life. His feet were bare, and his words penetrated to the
depth of the human soul."[7] Another alchemist describes the sun-child
"bedecked with purple on his throne."[8] The purple garment that the bridegroom describes comes from "thee and me," which is to say, the divine color
is generated not by either partner alone, but by their union. The union of the
masculine and feminine aspects of the divinity creates the incarnation of the
sun-child, or *filius*, and purple is his color and his emblem. But the signs of
exaltation are by no means over, for Thomas goes on:

> Thou shalt adorn me round about with shining and glittering
> gems and shalt cloth me with the garments of salvation and joy to
> overthrow the nations and all mine enemies, and shalt adorn me
> with a crown of gold engraved with the sign of holiness and shalt
> clothe me with a robe of righteousness and shalt betroth me with
> thy ring and clothe my feet in sandals of gold.[9]

The *coniunctio* creates in both partners, and in the alchemist, feelings of joy and salvation and produces once again cosmic regeneration. Through their harmonization as "glittering gems" around the marriage pair, the autonomy of the psychoidal powers is overthrown. The crown symbolizes the victory of the *lapis*, which is even called "crown of victory."[10] Gerald Dorn describes this stage as follows:

> Our Mercurius is therefore the same, who contains within him the perfections, virtues and powers of Sol, and who goes through the streets and houses of all the planets, and in his regeneration has obtained the power of Above and Below, wherefore he is to be likened to their marriage, as is evident from the white and the red that are conjoined in him. The sages have affirmed in their wisdom that all creatures are to be brought to one united substance.[11]

In the marriage of Sophia and God all the planets are also united, that is, all the psychoidal forces participate in this union. The crown therefore symbolizes the unity of the psychoid, and the fact that the *filius* is the newly empowered center of the psychoid. The bridegroom is indeed the holy of holies, for He now contains within Himself all the powers of the divine. The victory over chaos is achieved and the order of wisdom established.

The crown also refers to consciousness—here, it is a new consciousness created by the unity now established. The divine world, left to chaos, creates and fosters chaos at every level of being, and this chaos leads to evil and destruction, both at the individual and cosmic levels. Alchemy does not accept this state of things, but seeks the establishment of harmony and divine order, so that order prevails throughout the universe. "Order" does not mean rigidity, nor the order imposed by law or dictate; rather, order is the harmonious unfolding of Sophia, of the unimpaired flow of Wisdom that knows the place and function of all things. Consciousness—human and divine—based on the flow of Wisdom, is itself wise beyond measure and does not seek gain or undue profit, but for the right thing at the right time. Wisdom seeks to be Herself and to help all beings become themselves, and this is the order created when Sophia marries God and together they create the crown of victory.

The head is bedecked with the crown, while the feet are placed in golden sandals. From head to foot the transformation has occurred. The feet symbolize groundedness, and the shoes that the feet wear indicate the nature of the groundedness; the attitude toward the world in which one takes a stand. Sandals of gold indicate a divine viewpoint and the incarnation of the divinity. They indicate that the crown of consciousness is not only a heady thing, but is grounded now in actuality and substantial form. The *filius* is real and the union created is real. It is real not only in that the *filius* has taken on substance and form, but also because the alchemist experiences the reality of this new state as part of his or her own consciousness and as part of his or her relationship with the ally. The new birth created by the *coniunctio* is neither hope nor dream, but living truth.

The ecstatic love continues to flow from the voice of God who describes the beauty of His love and begs her to speak to Him, that is, to reveal her true nature to Him. The revelation of the nature of Sophia is overwhelming both to God and to Thomas, who struggles to contain his ecstasy and allow Sophia to speak through him. Accordingly, the voice changes from the voice of God to that of Sophia:

> I am the flower of the field and the lily of the valleys; I am the mother of fair love and [of fear and] of knowledge and of holy hope. As the fruitful vine I have brought forth a pleasant odour, and my flowers are the fruit of honour and riches. I am the bed of my beloved, which threescore of the most valiant ones surrounded, all holding swords upon their thigh because of fears in the night. I am all fair and there is no spot in me; looking through the windows, looking through the lattices of my beloved, wounding his heart with one of my eyes and with hair of my neck. I am the sweet smell of ointments giving an odour above all aromatical spices. . . . I am the most prudent virgin, coming forth as the Dawn, sing exceedingly, elect as the sun, fair as the moon, besides what is hid within.[12]

Sophia goes on in this wonderful passage, which is, in my opinion, the most complete description of her to be found anywhere. Flowers, and especially the lily, are important images. The Stone is like a flower that grows and blossoms as the alchemical work unfolds. The color often given to flowers represents the stages of the work, being black, white, or red. As Kelly puts it, at a certain point in the work, "flowers of all the colours of a Peacock's Tail begin to spring up in the Sage's vessel."[13] Holmyard tells us that the red elixir is called the flower of the sun.[14] Flowers very often symbolize feelings and the expression of feelings, as when one sends flowers to the sick or bereaved, or to brides and graduates. The power of the flower symbolism in alchemy indicates its feeling side. The creation of the Stone and the experience of the *coniunctio* is a feeling experience beyond description. I have written of the felt vision,[15] in which we feel to the core of our being the experience unfolding, and so it is in alchemy. Sophia bursts forth not as an intellectual understanding, but as a felt ecstatic vision, a knowing of knowledge, and a budding forth of wisdom. The experience of Sophia is a feeling experience, so that she is the flower, the feeling processes of alchemy.

So, too, is she the lily. No one uses the symbol of the lily more than Jacob Boehme, for whom it is the goal itself. He concludes the preface of his great work *On the Signature of Things* by saying it is the time to seek "for a lily blossoms upon the mountains and valleys in all the ends of the earth: He that seeketh findeth. Amen."[16] For Boehme, the lily is the divine within the human being and is the new person born in the light of God.[17] Titus Burckhardt comments that the lily corresponds to the quintessence.[18] The lily can be either white or red, and refers to the extracted and purified mercury or sulfur, respectively. At the same time, the white lily is feminine, and the red lily is masculine, so the lily itself can refer to the hermaphroditic nature of the Stone. Sophia is the lily as the divine, purified essence, and as the soul and feminine principle of all things, but she is the lily as partner of the hermaphrodite created in union with God. She is the sweet lily of Jacob Boehme, the divinized human soul or the divine essence within the human being.

Sophia is the vine that brings forth a pleasant odor. As the vine, she produces the grape and wine. George Ripley compares the flourishing of Noah's vineyard with the growth of the Stone.[19] Red wine is often compared with blood and the sap of the tree that becomes the Stone, and so relates to the vivifying power of the *anima mundi*. Sophia is the principle of growth within all nature and that which leads to transformation and incarnation. She creates that which is sweet, and in alchemy a good odor is the sign that the Stone is forming. The movement from a foul smell to a sweet one marks the movement from the *nigredo* to the *albedo* and even the *rubedo*.

All of these images point to the fecundity of Sophia and to her sweetness, as well as her beauty and numinosity. Bernard Trevisan remarks that the Stone, even in the white stage, exudes, "so sweet an odor that its like is not found in this World."[20] The otherworldly smell of the Stone is one of the signs of Its divinity.

Sophia is the bed of her beloved that is surrounded by sixty of the most valiant ones, all holding swords upon their thighs on account of the fears of the night. As von Franz correctly points out, the number sixty refers to the six planets (excluding the sun),[21] so that the image denotes the harmony and unity of the psychoidal forces created on the marriage bed, that is, through the *coniunctio* of Sophia and God. They are prepared for battle against the fears of the night, that is, fears of any remaining psychoidal forces not yet harmonized. I have mentioned a few times that there are many types of psychoidal forces, and while I do not wish to enter into a discussion of these varieties now, it should be noted that the planets, in my opinion, refer to divine forces that should be part of the *filius*, or harmonized by it, at least. There are other forces that might be likened to elementals or evil spirits that also exist in the psychoid, and the swords of the divine principles protect the alchemist and the Stone, Itself, from their influences. This passage serves as an interesting reminder that not all is yet brought into harmony in the psychoid, even when the *filius* born of the union of wisdom and power emerges.

Sophia says she is all fair and with no spot upon her, a sure sign of how far her transformation has progressed, for recall how she complained of being black and bespotted. Now she is pure and ready for union. She looks through the window into the body of her lover, another image of union. The window has several meanings, all of a very profound spiritual nature. Von Franz enumerates them in her commentary, indicating that the window symbolizes a connection between levels of reality, and with the connection of Wisdom to the highest spiritual power.[22] The window reveals the connection not only between Sophia and God, but between the spiritual world and the psychoid world, and the psychoid and the ordinary world. Sophia looks through the window, as if from her original spiritual place, to the psychoid place of her beloved, for as von Franz also notes, the lattices refers "to the soul penetrating the 'prison of the body.'"[23] That is, the spirit enters the physical, and so becomes psychoidal.

Sophia is the sweet smell of ointments giving an odor that is more beautiful than spices and perfume. Von Franz notes that the divine spirit is a perfume,[24] and Sophia is thus reminding us of her spiritual nature and beauty. In the outpouring of her description, Sophia thus offers us a picture of herself as a divine feminine power from whom blessings flow, and who is responsible for growth and transformation. She is the holy bride and the sweet smell of divinity; a goddess beyond compare.

But she is not finished with her self-exaltation. She describes not only her role in alchemy, but by so doing offers further insights into her nature:

> I am that land of the holy promise, which floweth with milk and honey and bringeth forth sweetest fruit in due season; wherefore

have all the philosophers commended me and sowed in me their
gold and silver and incombustible grain. And unless that grain
falling into me die, itself shall remain alone, but if it die, it bringeth
forth threefold fruit: for the first it shall bring forth shall be good
because it was sown in good earth, namely of pearls; the second
likewise good because it was sown in better earth, namely of leaves
[of silver,] and the third shall bring forth a thousand-fold because
it was sown in the best earth, namely of gold. For from the fruits of
this grain is made the food of life, which cometh down from
heaven. . . . I give and take not back, I feed and fail not, I make
secure and fear not; what more shall I say to my beloved? I am the
mediatrix of the elements, making one to agree with another; that
which is warm I make cold, and the reverse; that which is dry I
make moist, and the reverse; that which is hard I soften, and the
reverse. I am the end and my beloved is the beginning. I am the
whole work and all science is hidden in me.[25]

Sophia is establishing herself as a divine being, but more importantly, she is
declaring herself as the entire opus of alchemy. As the purified earth, she is
the goddess and the source of all life, but in the alchemical sense, she is the
mercurial body that receives all the seeds of the other metals and can
become those metals, or can help other metals take on their form. If silver
is added to her, she becomes silver; if gold, she becomes gold and, interestingly, if grain is added she multiplies it threefold. The grain is the food of
life that comes down from heaven. In these passages, Sophia is the vessel of
transformation, and anything added to her will transmute, and as the vessel
she receives the divine influx.

I mentioned earlier that the earth is the divine feminine principle.
What is added to her are the divine forms and emanations, which might be
likened to the masculine principle, so that the images speak yet again of the
coniunctio. This image is reminiscent of the Kabbalist notion that the
Shekinah receives the outpouring of all the higher Sephiroth and then
passes them into the world.

Moreover, I mentioned that one image for the completion of the work
is the changing of one element into another, and Sophia declares that she is
that which changes the elements into their opposites. We might understand
her comments by supposing she is describing not only her ability to transform all things, from the greatest to the lowest, but that she is the fundamental and divine earth of all things. To take on reality, to experience trans-

formation, we must be grounded in the feminine principle and its wisdom. Though Sophia becomes the body of the ally, the ally becomes her body, as well. The ally takes on deeper reality and substance, and in fact becomes more itself through grounding in the divine earth. She multiplies the power and substance not only of the ally, but all the psychoidal forces that come into relationship with her, for she is the principle of multiplication and nourishment. On the divine level, she feeds the forces of the psychoid and empowers them within that realm. On the human level, she is the source of nourishment for the soul, and through grounding ourselves in the divine feminine wisdom, we feed our soul and strengthen it in depth, quality, and breadth. The soul, too, is psychoidal, and is nourished by union with Sophia. In the imagery of the grain as nourishment for the soul, Thomas hints once more at immortality, for the grain, upon its death, is born again multiplied threefold.

Sophia unites all the opposites by changing them into each other, making the moist dry and the hot cold, and vice versa. This relates her to Mercurius and the psychological transcendent function that unites the opposites in the formation of the self. In all these ways, she forms the whole work of alchemy, which finds itself completely dependent on Sophia as the feminine principle. Unlike science, which emerged from the ruins of traditional alchemy, and which is so dedicated to masculine principles, alchemy must devote itself to the feminine in order to create the transformations that it seeks. The alchemists knew this and praised nature and the feminine time and again. Lyndy Abraham explains, "Alchemy sought to work *with* Nature, not conquer her. The alchemist used Nature's secrets as a blueprint for the processes of the opus."[26]

Sophia claims to be the whole work and, in fact, she is. She is the secret of the opus, for she is the soul of nature and the life of all life. Without her, nothing could live, not even a psychoidal being. All derive their life from her, and adding her to their own being increases their life force immeasurably. In addition, she is Wisdom, and Wisdom knows the nature of the work and how to succeed at it. Only those in harmony with her decrees can perform alchemy of any kind. She makes a further interesting statement when she declares that she is the end of the work and her beloved is the beginning. This statement comes immediately after she spoke of uniting the opposites, and here is a paradoxical reversal of roles that helps unite the opposites. As I have written all along, the divine masculine comes first, to be followed by the appearance and marriage with Sophia. Yet in this passage, we have seen her take the first priority to herself, and in her statement that she is the end of the work and God the beginning the ultimate reversal is reached. Yet paradoxically it is quite true, for God finds His fulfillment only in Sophia.

Psychoidal alchemy, through the union of the feminine and the masculine, creates the ally, as well as feeds and multiplies it through union with other psychoidal forces, and this may be accomplished only through the agency of Sophia. Furthermore, Sophia is the end of the work not only because she completes the ally, but also because she finds her own completion in the ally. Each finds in the other their own fulfillment and ultimate purpose and each without the other exists only in a partial sense.

Sophia is the goddess and she completes her equation with God when she declares in the next part of the parable that, "[I] will kill and I will make to live and there is none that can deliver out of my hand."[27] This quotation comes from Deut. 32:39, when God says: "See ye that I alone am, and there is no other God besides me; I will kill and I will make to live, I will strike and I will heal and there is none that can deliver out of my hand." Sophia is stating that she, too, alone is God.

I began this book with a quotation that the substance of the work is truly one, though it may appear in many forms or under many guises. The one true work is God and Sophia, for both are rooted in the one divine source. Yet, despite this oneness, we must be in awe of Sophia's claim for complete equality with the masculine God. As a psychoidal figure that has emerged from the divine root, she is no less than God, though her nature and function are different. She claims her right, indeed, as a divine hypostasis, as a goddess inferior to none. Only when her equality is fully recognized can the *coniunctio* occur. For that reason, the sentence that immediately follows her claim is:

> I stretch forth my mouth to my beloved and he presseth his to me; he and I are one; who shall separate us from love? None and no man, for our love is strong as death.[28]

I must admit I get chills whenever I read this line, not only for its ecstatic declaration of love, but because it is the revelation of the deepest secret of the godhead: the *mysterium coniunctionis* in which the two halves of God, separated since creation itself, are reunited not through power, nor will, nor force, but only and completely through love. Love is the mercurial glue that binds the godhead together in a new and more evolved form, for it is love between equals that unites God and Sophia in the *filius*. The masculine side of God is in awe of this union, too, for the voice in the chapter now shifts from Sophia to Him and He concludes the book in His paean of love:

O beloved, yea supremely beloved, thy voice hath sounded in my
ears, for it is sweet, and thine odour is above all aromatical spices.
O how comely is thy face, thy breasts more beautiful than wine, my
sister, my spouse, thy eyes are like the fishpools in Hesbon, thy
hairs are golden, thy cheeks are ivory, thy belly is as a round bowl
never wanting. . . . I will set my strength upon her and take hold of
her fruits and her breasts shall be as the clusters of wine. Come, my
beloved, and let us go into thy field . . . let us fill ourselves with
costly wine and ointments, and let no flower pass by us save we
crown ourselves therewith, first with lilies, then with roses. . . . Let
no meadow escape our riot . . . let us leave everywhere tokens of
joy, for this is our portion that we should live in the union of love
with joy and merriment. . .[29]

Thus the work is completed in Bacchanalian ecstasy and in the bliss of the
union of love and joy. The godhead celebrates its own reunification and the
alchemist shares in this bliss as best man and bridesmaid, tasting and knowing one aspect of the completion of God after another, for Sophia and God
built "three tabernacles, one for thee, a second for me, and a third for our
sons."[30] Sophia has found her place, God has found His place, and a place
has been created for their "sons," the alchemists themselves.

We live in a time when we stand at the edge of social and ecological disaster. Our world has provided little room for the feminine, and disregards the needs of beings other than humans. In our time, the Earth, far from being alive, is simply regarded as a source for our exploitation. Not only do we ignore the needs of the world as a physical organism, we ignore her soul and the soul of nature. We ignore our own souls as well and act for the most part as if they did not exist. We often treat others with slightly more contempt than we treat ourselves, and we ignore the needs of our neighbors as we ignore our own real needs.

There may no longer be any room for Sophia in a world such as the one we live in, but I hope there is. For if there is not, and we ignore the soul of the world and the inner voice of wisdom; if we ignore the quiet voice of uninvented truth, there may be no hope for us at all.

Sophia's message to me was that she and the other psychoidal beings are real. She asked me to demonstrate her reality and the fact that she needs both recognition and help. In this book I have tried to do so, being aware at all times of the difficulty of the task. I have tried to show that she is a living entity and an aspect of the divine world. Through knowing her, we come to know ourselves, and to know God as well. More even than knowing, we come to heal her, ourselves, and God.

Alchemy is an ancient tradition with many levels of meaning and possibilities of interpretation. I have found it most meaningful as a portrayal of the inner workings of the divinity and as a means of witnessing and so transforming psychoidal manifestations of that divinity. Alchemy remains alive today as an instrument for understanding and meaningfully intervening in the cosmic drama that unfolds around us, whether we notice it or not. Through its continued study we may learn more about this drama and the psychoidal beings that participate in it. Such learning may offer us a great opportunity to avoid disaster, as we come to realize just who we are and what our proper place in the scheme of things is. If we can learn this, and at the same time come to respect and honor the forces that surround us, we may be able to change the world.

Introduction

1. Jeffrey Raff, *Jung and the Alchemical Imagination* (Berwick, ME: Nicolas-Hays, 2000), and Jeffrey Raff and Linda Bonnington Vocatura, *Healing the Wounded God* (Berwick, ME: Nicolas-Hays, 2002).
2. Marie Louise von Franz, *The Aurora Consurgens: A Document Attributed to Thomas Aquinas on the Problem of Opposites in Alchemy* (Toronto: Inner City Press, 2000).
3. C. G. Jung, *Mysterium Coniunctionis, The Collected Works of C. G. Jung*, vol. 14, R. F. C. Hull, trans. Bollingen Series XX (Princeton: Princeton University Press, 1977).
4. Nathan Schwartz-Salant, *The Mystery of Human Relationship: Alchemy and the Transformation of the Self* (New York: Routledge, 1998), p. 13

Chapter 1

1. Gerald T. Elmore, *Islamic Sainthood in the Fullness of Time* (Boston: Brill, 1999), p. 301.
2. "Mind to Hermes" in Brian P. Copenhaver, trans., *Hermetica* (Cambridge: Cambridge University Press, 1996), p. 41.
3. "Definitions of Asclepius to King Ammon on god, matter, vice, fate, the sun intellectual essence, divine essence, mankind, the arrangement of the plenitude, the seven stars, and mankind according to the image" in Copenhaver, *Hermetica*, p. 60.
4. Elmore, *Islamic Sainthood*, p. 332.
5. Zohar, Harry Sperling and Maurice Simon, trans. (London, Jeruselum, New York: The Soncino Press, 1973), Bereshith, § 1, p. 101a
6. William C. Chittick, *The Sufi Path of Knowledge* (New York: State University of New York Press, 1989), p. 346.
7. Elmore, *Islamic Sainthood*, p. 325.
8. For a fuller discussion of the views of Paracelsus and Boehme concerning fantasy, see Raff, *Jung and the Alchemical Imagination* (Berwick, ME: Nicolas-Hays, 2000), p. 40 ff.
9. For a detailed discussion of the role of Names in the writings of Ibn Arabi, see William C. Chittick, *The Sufi Path of Knowledge* (New York: State University of New York Press, 1989).
10. Jacob Boehme, *The Confessions of Jacob Boehme* (Kila, MT: Kessinger, n.d.), p. 97.

Chapter 2

1. David Winston, ed., *The Wisdom of Solomon: The Anchor Bible, vol. 43* (New York: Doubleday, 1979), pp. 178, 184.

2. Winston, *Wisdom of Solomon*, p. 191.

3. G. R. S. Mead, *Simon Magus: The Gnostic Magician* (Edmonds, WA: Holmes, n.d.), p. 6.

4. Mead, *Simon Magus*, p. 39. "Epinoia" and Ennoia" are two of the many names for Sophia in Gnosticism.

5. James M. Robinson, general editor, *The Nag Hammadi Library* (San Francisco: HarperSanFrancisco, 1977), p. 101.

6. "The Apocryphon of John" in Robinson, *The Nag Hammadi Library*, p. 111.

7. "The Apocryphon of John" in Robinson, *The Nag Hammadi Library*, p. 114.

8. Henry Khunrath, *A Naturall Chymicall Symbolum or a short confession of Henry Kunwrath of Lipsicke Doctor of Phisick Concerning ye universal, naturale Triune, wonderous, marvellous operacion of ye most misticall Naturale Chaos of Alchimie*, MS. Ashmole 1459 (The Alchemy Web Site, www.levity.com/alchemy/khunconf.html) p. 103.

9. Andrew Weeks, *Paracelsus* (Albany: State University of New York Press, 1997), p. 83.

10. Weeks, *Paracelsus*, p. 127.

11. C. G. Jung, *Aion*, Collected Works of C. G. Jung, Vol 9ii, R. F. C. Hull, trans., Bollingen Series XX (Princeton: Princeton University Press, 1970), ¶ 185.

12. Marie-Louise von Franz, *Alchemy* (Toronto: Inner City Books, 1980), p. 236.

13. Winston, *The Wisdom of Solomon*, p. 185.

14. Jean Chevalier and Alain Gheerbrant, *The Penguin Dictionary of Symbols*, John Buchanan-Brown, trans. (London: Penguin Books, 1996), p. 661

15. Anonymous, "Nature Discovered," in *Alchemical Compendium, Hermetic Studies*, vol. 3 (Glasgow: Adam McLean, 1991), p. 82.

16. Winston, *The Wisdom of Solomon*, p. 184.

17. Winston, *The Wisdom of Solomon*, p. 191.

18. C. G. Jung, *Psychology and Alchemy, The Collected Works of C. G. Jung*, vol. 12, R. F. C. Hull, trans., Bollingen Series XX (Princeton: Princeton University Press, 1977), ¶ 420.

19. Michael Maier, *Atalanta Fugiens*, Joscelyn Godwin, trans. and ed. (Grand Rapids, MI: Phanes Press, 1989), p. 157.

20. Alexander Roob, *Alchemy and Mysticism* (New York: Taschen, 1997), p. 502.

21. Andrea De Pascalis, *Alchemy: The Golden Art* (Rome: Gremese International, 1995), p. 175.

22. Roob, *Alchemy and Mysticism*, p. 239.

23. Jacob Boehme, *The Way to Christ, The Classics of Western Spirituality Series*, Peter Erb, trans. (New York: Paulist Press, 1978), p. 59.

24. Cyliani, *Hermes Unveiled*, Patrick J. Smith, trans. (Edmonds, WA: Holmes, 1997), p. 11.

25. Winston, *Wisdom of Solomon*, p. 167.

26. Johann Harprecht, *Treatise of Salt*, Patrick J. Smith, trans. (Edmonds, WA: Holmes, 2000), p. 26.

27. Boehme, *Way to Christ*, p. 17.

28. Lyndy Abraham, *A Dictionary of Alchemical Imagery* (Cambridge: Cambridge University Press, 1998), p. 178.

29. Henry Khunrath, *A Naturall Chymicall Symbolum*, MS Ashmole 1459 (Alchemy Web Site, www.levity.com/alchemy/khunconf.html) p. 3.

30. C. G. Jung, *Mysterium Coniunctionis, Collected Works of C. G. Jung*, vol. 14, R. F. C. Hull, trans., Bollingen Series XX (Princeton: Princeton University Press, 1970) ¶ 327. Further reference to this work will be cited as CW 14.

31. Jung, CW 14, ¶ 327.
32. Jung, CW 14, ¶ 328.
33. Jung, CW 14, ¶ 533.
34. Jacob Boehme, *The Three Principles of the Divine Essence* (Chicago: Yogi Publication Co., 1909), p. 378.
35. Jacob Boehme, *The Key,* William Law, trans. (Grand Rapids, MI: Phanes Press, 1991), p. 23.
36. Boehme, *The Three Principles,* p. 378.
37. Weeks, *Paracelsus,* p. 150.
38. Simon Forman, *Of the Division of Chaos* (Alchemy Web Site, www.levity.com/alchemy/forman_chaos.html), p. 11.
39. Ibid.
40. Artephius, *The Secret Book* (Alchemy Web Site, www.levity.com/alchemy/artephiu.html), ¶ 18.

Chapter 3

1. Marie-Louise von Franz, ed. *Aurora Consurgens: A Document Attributed to Thomas Aquinas on the Problem of Opposites in Alchemy* (Toronto: Inner City Books, 2000), p. 33. Because of the frequency with which I shall quote from this text I shall refer to it henceforth simply as *Aurora.*
2. *Aurora,* p. 158.
3. Zech. 9:14.
4. *Aurora,* p. 159.
5. A. E. Waite, ed., *The Turba Philosophorum* (New York: Samuel Weiser, 1976), p. 163.
6. Eirenaeus Philalethes, *The Fount of Chemical Truth* (Alchemy Web Site, www.levity.com/alchemy/phila3.html), ¶ 8.
7. *Hermaphrodite Child of the Sun and Moon,* Mike Brenner, trans. (Alchemy Web Site, www.levity.com/alchemy/hermoz.html, translation copyright © Mike Brenner, 1997), § II, ¶ 2.
8. Sigismund Bacstrom, *Rosicrucian Aphorisms and Process* (Alchemy Web Site, www.levity.com/alchemy/bacsproc.html), ¶ 1.
9. Bacstrom, *Rosicrucian Aphorism,* ¶ 2.
10. Jung, CW 14, ¶ 372.
11. Anonymous, "The Sophic Hydrolith or The Waterstone of the Wise" in Arthur Edward Waite, ed., *The Hermetic Museum* (York Beach, ME: Weiser, 1994), p. 78.
12. *Aurora,* p. 33.
13. *Aurora,* pp. 33-35.
14. Anonymous, "The Glory of the World" in Waite, ed., *The Hermetic Museum,* p. 180.
15. "Tabula Smaragdina" from *The Geheime figuren,* (Alchemy Web Site, www.levity.com/alchemy/emer_gf.html), lines 165–170.
16. Martinus Rulandus, *A Lexicon of Alchemy* (Reprint: Kila, MT: Kessinger, n.d.), p. 353.
17. *Aurora,* p. 35.
18. Henry Corbin, *The Man of Light in Iranian Sufism* (New Lebanon, NY: Omega Publications, 1994).
19. Anonymous, *The Natural Round Physick or Philosophy of the Alchymical Cabalistical Vision* (Alchemy Web Site, www.levity.com/alchemy/alchcab.html), ¶ 3.

20. C. G. Jung, *Alchemical Studies, The Collected Works of C. G. Jung,* vol. 13, R. F. C. Hull, trans., Bollingen Series XX (Princeton: Princeton University Press, 1970), ¶ 162.

21. "Waterstone of the Wise," in Waite, ed., *The Hermetic Museum,* p. 71.

22. "Glory of the World," in Waite, ed., *The Hermetic Museum,* p. 38.

23. Quoted in R.W. Councell, *Apollogia Alchymia* (London: John M. Watkins, 1925), p. 5.

24. A Lover of Philalethes, *A Short Enquiry concerning the Hermetick art* (London: 1714, Alchemy Web Site, www.levity.com/alchemy/shortenq.html), p. 2.

25. Johannes Helmond, *Alchemy Unveiled,* Gerhard Hanswille and Deborah Brumlich, trans. (Salt Lake City: Merkur, 1999) p. 25.

26. Anonymous, *An hundred aphorisms containing the whole body of magic,* MS. Sloane 1321, Adam McLean, trans. (Alchemy Web Site, www.levity.com/alchemy/100aphor.html) aphorism 41.

27. C. G. Jung, *Alchemical Studies,* ¶ 459.

28. *Turba Philosophorum,* pp. 175–176.

29. Cyliani, *Hermes Unveiled,* Patrick J. Smith, trans. (Edmonds, WA: Holmes, 1997), p. 10.

30. For example, see Ali Puli, *The Center of Nature Concentrated* (Edmonds, WA: The Alchemical Press, 1988), p. 21.

31. *Aurora,* p.165.

32. Dennis William Hauck, *The Emerald Tablet* (New York: Penguin Arkana, 1999), p. 110.

33. *Nodus Sophicus Enodatus,* quoted in Sigismund Bacstrom, *Bacstrom's Alchemical Anthology,* J. W. Hamilton-Jones, ed. (Reprint: Kila, MT: Kessinger, n.d.), p. 55.

34. "The Waterstone of the Wise," p. 82.

35. In chapter 1, I cited text from the Gnostics, who often likened Wisdom to fire, and the same is obviously true in alchemy.

36. Anonymous, *Aurea Catena Homeri: The Golden Chain of Homerus,* Sigismund Bacstrom, trans. (San Francisco: Sapere Aude Metaphysical Republishers, 1983), p. 2.

37. Jean d'Espagnet, *The Hermetic Arcanum* (Edmonds, WA: The Alchemical Press, 1988), p. 37.

38. Thomas Vaughan, "Coelum Terrae," in A. E. Waite, ed., *The Magical Writings of Thomas Vaughan* (Reprint: Kila, MT: Kessinger, n.d.), p. 127.

39. Vaughan, "Coelum Terrae," in Waite, *The Magical Writings of Thomas Vaughan,* p. 142.

40. *Aurora,* p. 39.

41. *Aurora,* p. 39 n. 22. Brackets are von Franz's.

42. *Aurora,* p. 173.

43. *Aurora,* p. 39.

44. Edward Kelly, "The Stone of the Philosophers" in A. E. Waite, ed., *The Alchemical Writings of Edward Kelly* (New York: Samuel Weiser 1976), p. 35.

Chapter 4

1. *Aurora,* p. 45.

2. *Aurora,* p. 51.

3. Ibid.

4. *Aurora,* p. 51 n. 4.

5. *Aurora,* p. 55. Angle brackets are von Franz's interpolation.

6. *Aurora,* p. 212.

7. E. J. Holmyard, *Alchemy* (New York: Dover, 1990), p. 149.

8. Jung, *CW* 14, ¶ 6.

9. Jung, *CW* 13, ¶ 85.

10. "The Glory of the World," in A. E. Waite, ed., *The Hermetic Museum* (York Beach, ME: Weiser, 1994), p. 173.

11. Jung, *CW* 13, ¶ 106.

12. *Aurora*, p. 55

Chapter 5

1. *Aurora*, pp. 219–220.

2. Anonymous, *Treasury of the Sages*, quoted in Edward Kelly, *The Stone of the Philosophers*, in A. E.. Waite, ed., *The Alchemical Writings of Edward Kelly* (New York: Samuel Weiser, 1976), pp. 42–43.

3. *Aurora*, p. 57.

4. Lyndy Abraham, *A Dictionary of Alchemical Imagery* (Cambridge: Cambridge University Press, 1998), p. 42.

5. *The Book of Komarios* quoted in Marie-Louise von Franz, *On Dreams and Death* (Chicago: Open Court, 1998), pp. 28–29.

6. *Aurora*, pp. 57–59.

7. *Aurora*, p. 59.

8. *Aurora*, p. 237.

9. *Aurora*, p. 63.

10. *Aurora*, p. 65.

11. *Aurora*, p. 239

12. At the time the *Aurora* was written, astronomers had discovered only seven "planets": the Sun, the Moon, Mercury, Mars, Venus, Jupiter, and Saturn.

13. Titus Burckhardt, *Alchemy*, William Stoddart, trans. (Louisville: Fons Vitae, 1997), p.192.

14. *Aurora*, p. 63.

15. *Aurora*, p. 59 n. 11.

16. *Ibid.*

17. *Ibid.*

18. *Aurora*, p. 59.

19. Martinus Rulandus, *A Lexicon of Alchemy* (Reprint: Kila, MT: Kessinger, n.d.), p. 207.

20. Quoted in Abraham, *A Dictionary of Alchemical Imagery*, p. 10.

21. George Ripley, "Twelve Gates," from *The Compound of Alchymy*, 1591 edition modernized by Adam McLean (Alchemy Web Site, www.levity.com/alchemy/ripgat2.html), ¶ 5.

22. Edward Kelly, *The Theater of Terrestrial Astronomy* in Waite, ed., *The Alchemical Writings of Edward Kelly*, p. 138.

23. Abraham, *A Dictionary of Alchemical Imagery*, p. 98.

Chapter 6

1. *Aurora*, p. 67.

2. *Ibid.*

3. *Aurora*, p. 246.

4. Anonymous, *The Chemical Wedding of Christian Rosenkreutz: Magnum Opus Hermetic Sourceworks*, Joselyn Godwin, trans. (Grand Rapids, MI: Phanes Press, 1991), pp. 74–75.

5. Cyliani, *Hermes Unveiled*, Patrick J. Smith, trans. (Edmonds, WA: Holmes, 1997), p. 35 fn.

6. Nicholas Flammel, *Alchemical Hieroglyphics* (Berkeley Heights: Heptangle Books, n.d.), p. 13.

7. Titus Burckhardt, *Alchemy*, William Stoddart, trans. (Louisville: Fons Vitae, 1997), pp. 175–176.

8. Thomas Vaughan, "Coelum Terrae," in A. E. Waite, ed., *The Magical Writings of Thomas Vaughan*, p. 129.

9. *Aurora*, p. 69.

10. *Aurora*, p. 71.

11. *Aurora*, p. 69.

12. *Aurora*, p. 71.

13. *Ibid.*

14. Titus Burckhardt, *Alchemy*, p. 47.

15. George Ripley, "Twelve Gates," from *The Compound of Alchymy*, 1591 edition modernized by Adam McLean (Alchemy Web Site, www.levitiy.com/alchemy/ripgat6.html), ¶ 12.

16. Joscelyn Godwin, trans., *The Chemical Wedding of Christian Rosenkreutz* (Grand Rapids, MI: Phanes Press, 1992), p. 93.

17. Edward Kelly, "The Stone of the Philosophers," in A. E. Waite, ed., *The Alchemical Writings of Edward Kelly* (New York: Samuel Weiser, 1976), p. 43.

18. "The Glory of the World," in A. E. Waite, ed., *The Hermetic Museum* (York Beach, ME: Weiser, 1994), p. 232.

19. Quoted in E. J. Holmyard, *Alchemy* (New York: Dover, 1990), p. 147

20. Thomas Vaughan, "Coelum Terrae," in Waite, ed., *Magical Writings of Thomas Vaughan*, p. 147.

21. Jung, *CW* 14, ¶ 718.

Chapter 7

1. *Aurora*, pp. 73, 75.

2. *Aurora*, pp. 270, 273.

3. *Aurora*, p. 75.

4. Jung, *CW* 14, ¶ 757.

5. Jung, *CW* 14, ¶ 758.

6. A. E. Waite, ed., *The Hermetic and Alchemical Writings of Paracelsus*, (Kila MT: Kessinger, n.d.), I: 117 fn.

7. *The Emerald Tablet*, translation from Latin in Steele and Singer 1928: 492 (Alchemy Web Site, www.levity.com/alchemy/emerald.html), ¶ 8.

8. *Aurora*, p. 77.

9. *Aurora*, pp. 77, 79.

10. *Aurora*, p. 79.

11. *Aurora*, p. 275.

Chapter 8

1. *Aurora*, pp. 87, 89.
2. *Aurora*, p. 87.
3. *Aurora*, p. 89.
4. *Ibid.*
5. *Aurora*, pp. 89, 91.
6. *Aurora*, p. 91.
7. *Ibid.*
8. *Ibid.*
9. *Aurora*, p. 93.
10. *Ibid.*
11. George Ripley, "Twelve Gates," from *The Compound of Alchymy*, 1591 edition modernized by Adam McLean (Alchemy Web Site, www.levity.com/alchemy/ripgat10.html), p. 43.
12. *Aurora*, p. 95.
13. *Ibid.*
14. *Aurora*, pp. 95, 97.
15. *Aurora*, p. 99

Chapter 9

1. *Aurora*, p. 101.
2. *Aurora*, p. 314
3. A. E. Waite, ed., *Turba Philosophorum* (New York: Samuel Weiser, 1976), pp. 175–176.
4. *Aurora*, p. 103.
5. Quoted in Jung, *CW* 13, ¶ 87.
6. *Aurora*, p. 103.
7. *Ibid.*
8. *Aurora*, p. 327.
9. *Aurora*, p. 105.
10. *Aurora*, p. 320.
11. *Aurora*, p. 107.
12. Jacob Boehme, *The Confessions of Jacob Boehme* (Reprint: Kila, MT: Kessinger, n.d.), pp. 128–129.
13. *Aurora*, p. 107.
14. *Aurora*, p. 109.
15. *Ibid.*
16. *Aurora*, p. 333.
17. *Aurora*, p. 109.
18. *Aurora*, p. 111.
19. *Ibid.*
20. Edward Kelly, "The Stone of the Philosophers," in A. E. Waite, ed., *The Alchemical Writings of Edward Kelly* (New York: Samuel Weiser, 1976), p. 12.
21. Alexandre Toussaint de Limojon, Sieur de Saint-Didier, *A Letter to the True Disciples of Hermes* (Alchemy Web Site, www.levity.com/alchemy/didier.html), ¶ 3.

22. *Aurora,* p. 111.
23. *Aurora,* p. 113.
24. *Ibid.*
25. *Ibid.*
26. *Aurora,* p. 115.
27. *Ibid.*
28. *Aurora,* pp. 115, 117.
29. Ripley, "The Fourth Gate, in *The Compound of Alchymy* (Alchemy Web Site, www.levity.com/alchemy/ripgat4.html), ¶ 4.
30. *Aurora,* pp. 117, 119.
31. Titus Burckhardt, *Alchemy,* William Stoddart, trans. (Louisville: Fons Vitae, 1997), p 28.
32. Joseph Needham, *Science and Civilization in China,* volume V: 4 (Cambridge: Cambridge University Press, 1992), p. 244.
33. Needham, *Science and Civilization in China,* p. 245. Brackets are mine.
34. *Aurora,* p. 338.

Chapter 10

1. *Aurora,* p. 340.
2. Henry Corbin, *Avicenna and the Visionary Recital,* Willard R. Trask, trans., Bollingen Series LXVI (Princeton: Princeton University Press, 1990) pp. 47–48.
3. *Aurora,* p. 121.
4. *Ibid.*
5. *Aurora,* p. 123.
6. David Gordon White, *The Alchemical Body* (Chicago: Chicago University Press, 1996), p. 285.
7. A. E. Waite, *Hermetic and Alchemical Writings of Paracelsus* (Reprint: Kila, MT: Kessinger, n.d.), Part 1, p. 121.
8. Jung, *CW* 14, ¶ 319.
9. Bernard Trevisan, *The Abandoned Word,* Patrick J. Smith, trans. (Edmonds, WA: Holmes, 1999), p. 17.
10. Anonymous, *Book of Alze* (Alchemy Web Site, www.levity.com/alchemy/alze.html), ¶ 3.
11. *Aurora,* p. 121.
12. Lyndy Abraham, *A Dictionary of Alchemical Imagery* (Cambridge: Cambridge University Press, 1998), p. 74.
13. *Aurora,* pp. 125, 127.
14. *The Secret Book of Artephius* (Alchemy Web Site, www.levity.com/alchemy/artephiu.html), ¶ 15.
15. *Aurora,* p. 127.
16. *Aurora,* p. 129.

Chapter 11

1. *Aurora,* p. 133.
2. *Aurora,* pp. 133, 135.
3. *Aurora,* p. 135.

4. *Aurora*, pp. 135, 137.

5. *Aurora*, p. 371.

6. *Ibid.*

7. Basil Valentine, *Twelve Keys* (Alchemy Web Site, www.levity.com/alchemy/twelvkey.html), ¶ 38.

8. *Hermaphrodite child of the Sun and Moon*, Mike Brenner, trans. (Alchemy Web Site, www.levity.com/alchemy/herm01.html, 1997), § I, ¶ 1.

9. *Aurora*, p.137.

10. Jung, *CW* 14, ¶ 12.

11. Gerald Dorn, *Congeries Paracelsicae chemicae*, quoted in Jung, *CW* 14, ¶ 12.

12. *Aurora*, p. 139.

13. Edward Kelly, *The Theatre of Terrestrial Astronomy*, in A. E. Waite, ed., *The Alchemical Writings of Edward Kelly* (New York: Samuel Weiser, 1976), p. 8.

14. E. J. Holmyard, *Alchemy* (New York: Dover, 1990), p. 144.

15. Jeffrey Raff, "The Felt Vision," in Donald F. Sandner and Steven H. Wong, eds., *The Sacred Heritage* (New York: Routledge, 1997).

16. Jacob Boehme, *The Signature of all Things* (Reprint: Kila, MT: Kessinger, n.d.), p.8.

17. Franz Hartmann, *The Life and Doctrines of Jacob Boehme* (Reprint: Kila, MT: Kessinger, n.d.), p. 276.

18. Titus Burckhardt, *Alchemy*, p. 112.

19. George Ripley, "The Fifth Gate," in *The Compound of Alchymy* (Alchemy Web Site, www.levity.com/alchemy/ripgat5.html) ¶ 13.

20. Bernard Trevisan, *The Abandoned Word*, Patrick J. Smith, trans. (Edmonds, WA: Holmes, 1999), p. 5.

21. *Aurora*, p. 378.

22. *Aurora*, p. 379.

23. *Ibid.*

24. *Ibid.*

25. *Aurora*, pp. 141, 143.

26. Lyndy Abraham, *A Dictionary of Alchemical Imagery* (Cambridge: Cambridge University Press, 1998), p. 49.

27. *Aurora*, p. 143.

28. *Aurora*, p. 145.

29. *Aurora*, pp. 145, 147.

30. *Aurora*, p. 147.

Abraham, Lyndy. *A Dictionary of Alchemical Imagery*. Cambridge: Cambridge University Press, 1998.

Anonymous. "The Glory of the World." In Arthur Edward Waite, ed., *The Hermetic Museum*. York Beach, ME: Weiser, 1994.

Anonymous. "The Sophic Hydrolith or The Waterstone of the Wise." In Arthur Edward Waite, ed., *The Hermetic Museum*. York Beach, ME: Weiser, 1994.

Anonymous. *Book of Alze*. Alchemy Web Site, www.levity.com/alchemy/alze.html.

Anonymous. *The Natural Round Physick or Philosophy of the Alchymical Cabalistical Vision*. Alchemy Web Site, www.levity.com/alchemy/alchcab.html.

Artephius. *The Secret Book*. Alchemy Web Site, www.levity.com/alchemy/artephiu.html.

Bacstrom, Sigismund. *Rosicrucian Aphorisms and Process*. Alchemy Web Site, www.levity.com/alchemy/bacsproc.html.

Bacstrom, Sigismund trans. *Aurea Catena Homeri: The Golden Chain of Homerus*. San Francisco: Sapere Aude Metaphysical Republishers, 1983.

Boehme, Jacob *The Confessions of Jacob Boehme*. Reprint: Kila, MT: Kessinger, n.d.

———. *The Key*. William Law, trans. Grand Rapids, MI: Phanes Press, 1991.

———. *The Signature of all Things*. Reprint: Kila, MT: Kessinger, n.d.

———. *The Three Principles of the Divine Essence*. Chicago: Yogi Publication Co., 1909.

———. *The Way to Christ: The Classics of Western Spirituality Series*. Peter Erb, trans. New York: Paulist Press, 1978.

Brenner, Mike, trans. *Hermaphrodite Child of the Sun and Moon*. Alchemy Web Site, www.levity.com/alchemy/hermaph.html. Translation copyright © Mike Brenner, 1997.

Burckhardt, Titus. *Alchemy*. William Stoddart, trans. Louisville: Fons Vitae, 1997.

Chevalier, Jean and Alain Gheerbrant. *The Penguin Dictionary of Symbols*. John Buchanan-Brown, trans. London: Penguin Books, 1996.

Chittick, William C. *The Sufi Path of Knowledge*. New York: State University of New York Press, 1989.

Copenhaver, Brian P., trans. *Hermetica*. Cambridge: Cambridge University Press, 1996.

Corbin, Henry. *Avicenna and the Visionary Recitak*. Willard R. Trask, trans., Bollingen Series LXVI. Princeton: Princeton University Press, 1990.

———. *The Man of Light in Iranian Sufism*. New Lebanon: Omega Publications, 1994.

Councell, R. W. *Apollogia Alchymia*. London: John M. Watkins, 1925.

Cyliani. *Hermes Unveiled*. Patrick J. Smith, trans. Edmonds, WA: Holmes, 1997.

De Mehung, Jean. *The Remonstrance of Nature*. In Waite, A. E., ed., *The Hermetic Museum*. York Beach, ME: Weiser, 1991.

De Pascalis, Andrea. *Alchemy: The Golden Art*. Rome: Gremese International, 1995.

d'Espagnet, Jean. *The Hermetic Arcanum*. Edmonds, WA: The Alchemical Press, 1988.

Dorn, Gerald. *Congeries Paracelsicae chemicae*. Quoted in C. G. Jung, *Mysterium Coniunctionis, The Collected Works of C. G. Jung*, vol. 14. R. F. C. Hull, trans. Bollingen Series XX. Princeton: Princeton University Press, 1977.

Elmore, Gerald T. *Islamic Sainthood in the Fullness of Time*. Boston: Brill, 1999.

Emerald Tablet, The. Translation from Latin in Steel and Singer 1928: 492. Alchemy Web Site, www.levity.com/alchemy/emerald.html.

Flammel, Nicholas. *Alchemical Hieroglyphics*. Berkeley Heights, CA: Heptangle Books, n.d.

Forman, Simon. *Of the Division of Chaos*. Alchemy Web Site, www.levity.com/alchemy/forman_chaos.html.

Godwin, Joscelyn, trans. *The Chemical Wedding of Christian Rosenkreutz*. Grand Rapids, MI: Phanes Press.

Harprecht, Johann. *Treatise of Salt*. Patrick J. Smith, trans. Edmonds, WA: Holmes, 2000.

Hartmann, Franz. *The Life and Doctrines of Jacob Boehme*. Reprint: Kila, MT: Kessinger, n.d.

Hauck, Dennis William. *The Emerald Tablet*. New York: Penguin Arkana, 1999.

Helmond, Johannes. *Alchemy Unveiled*. Gerhard Hanswille and Deborah Brumlich, trans. Salt Lake City: Merkur, 1999.

Holmyard, E. J. *Alchemy*. New York: Dover, 1990.

Jung, C. G. *Aion, The Collected Works of C. G. Jung*, vol 9ii, R.F.C. Hull, trans., Bollingen Series XX. Princeton: Princeton University Press, 1970).

———. *Alchemical Studies, The Collected Works of C. G. Jung*, vol. 13, R.F.C. Hull, trans., Bollingen Series XX. Princeton : Princeton University Press, 1970.

———. *Mysterium Coniuncitionis, The Collected Works of C. G. Jung*, vol. 14, R.F.C. Hull, trans., Bollingen Series XX. Princeton: Princeton University Press, 1970.

———. *Psychology and Alchemy, The Collected Works of C. G. Jung*, vol. 12, R.F.C. Hull, trans., Bollingen Series XX. Princeton: Princeton University Press, 1977.

Kelly, Edward. "The Stone of the Philosophers." In Arthur Edward Waite, ed., *The Alchemical Writings of Edward Kelly*. New York: Samuel Weiser, 1976.

———. "The Theater of Terrestrial Astronomy." In Arthur Edward Waite, ed., *The Alchemical Writings of Edward Kelly*. New York: Samuel Weiser, 1976.

Khunrath, Henry. *A Naturall Chymicall Symbolum*, MS. Ashmole 1459. Alchemy Web Site, www.levity.com/alchemy/khunconf.html.

Maier, Michael. *Atalanta Fugiens*. Joscelyn Godwin, trans. and ed. Grand Rapids, MI: Phanes Press, 1989.

McLean, Adam trans. *An hundred aphorisms containing the whole body of magic*. MS. Sloane 1321. Alchemy Web Site, www.levity.com/alchemy/100aphor.html.

Mead, G.R.S. *Simon Magus: The Gnostic Magician*. Edmonds, WA: Holmes, n.d.

Needham, Joseph. *Science and Civilization in China*, volume V: 4. Cambridge: Cambridge University Press, 1992.

Nodus Sophicus Enodatus. Quoted in Bacstrom, Sigismund, *Bacstrom's Alchemical Anthology*. J. W. Hamilton-Jones, ed. Reprint: Kila, MT: Kessinger, n.d.

Philalethes, A Lover of. *A Short Enquiry concerning the Hermetick art.* London: 1714. Alchemy Web Site, www.levity.com/alchemy/ shortenq.html.

Philalethes, Eirenaeus. *The Fount of Chemical Truth.* Alchemy Web Site, www.levity.com/alchemy/philal3.html.

Puli, Ali. *The Center of Nature Concentrated.* Edmonds, WA: The Alchemical Press, 1988.

Raff, Jeffrey. "The Felt Vision." In Sandner, Donald F. and Steven H. Wong, eds. *The Sacred Heritage.* New York: Routledge, 1997.

———. *Jung and the Alchemical Imagination.* Berwick, ME: Nicolas-Hays, 2000.

Raff, Jeffrey and Linda Bonnington Vocatura. *Healing the Wounded God.* Berwick, ME: Nicolas-Hays, 2002.

Ripley, George. *The Compound of Alchymy.* 1591 edition modernized by Adam McLean. Alchemy Web Site, www.levity.com/alchemy/ ripgat2.html.

Robinson, James M., ed. *The Nag Hammadi Library.* San Francisco: HarperSanFrancisco, 1977.

Roob, Alexander. *The Hermetic Museum: Alchemy and Mysticism.* New York: Tashen, 1997.

Rulandus, Martinus. *A Lexicon of Alchemy.* Reprint: Kila, MT: Kessinger, n.d.

Saint-Didier, Alexandre Toussaint de Limojon, Sieur de. *A Letter to the True Disciples of Hermes.* Mike Dickman, trans. Paris, 1688. Alchemy Web Site, www.levity.com/alchemy/didier.html.

Schwartz-Salant, Nathan. *The Mystery of Human Relationship: Alchemy and the Transformation of the Self.* New York: Routledge, 1998.

Tabula Smaragdina. From the *Geheime figuren.* Alchemy Web Site, www.levity.com/alchemy/emer_gf.html.

Treasury of the Sages. Quoted in Kelly, Edward, "The Stone of the Philosophers." In Arthur Edward Waite, ed. *The Alchemical Writings of Edward Kelly.* New York: Samuel Weiser, 1976.

Trevisan, Bernard. *The Abandoned Word,* Patrick J. Smith, trans. Edmonds, WA: Holmes.

Valentine, Basil *Twelve Keys.* Alchemy Web Site, www.levity.com/alchemy/ twelvkey.html.

Vaughan, Thomas "Coelum Terrae." In Arthur Edward Waite, ed., *The Magical Writings of Thomas Vaughan.* Reprint: Kila, MT: Kessinger, n.d.

Von Franz, Marie-Louise. *Alchemy.* Toronto: Inner City Books, 1980.

———. *On Dreams and Death.* Chicago: Open Court, 1998.

Von Franz, Marie-Louise, ed. *The Aurora Consurgens: A Document Attributed to Thomas Aquinas on the Problem of Opposites in Alchemy.* Toronto: Inner City Press, 2000.

Waite, Arthur Edward, ed. *The Alchemical Writings of Edward Kelly.* New York: Samuel Weiser, 1976.

———. *The Hermetic and Alchemical Writings of Paracelsus.* Reprint: Kila, MT: Kessinger, n.d.

———. *The Turba Philosophorum.* New York: Samuel Weiser, 1976.

Weeks, Andrew. *Paracelsus.* Albany: State University of New York Press, 1997.

White, David Gordon. *The Alchemical Body.* Chicago: Chicago University Press, 1996.

Winston, David, ed. *The Wisdom of Solomon: The Anchor Bible,* vol. 43. New York: Doubleday, 1979.

Zohar. Harry Sperling and Maurice Simon, trans. London, Jerusalem, New York: The Soncino Press, 1973.

INDEX